Their Best Behavior

Their Best Behavior

Practical Strategies for 10 Common Classroom Challenges

Allie Szczecinski, M. Ed.

JB JOSSEY-BASS™
A Wiley Brand

Copyright © 2025 by John Wiley & Sons, Inc. All rights reserved, including rights for text and data mining and training of artificial technologies or similar technologies.

Jossey-Bass, a Wiley imprint

Published by John Wiley & Sons, Inc., Hoboken, New Jersey.
Published simultaneously in Canada.

No part of this publication may be reproduced, stored in a retrieval system, or transmitted in any form or by any means, electronic, mechanical, photocopying, recording, scanning, or otherwise, except as permitted under Section 107 or 108 of the 1976 United States Copyright Act, without either the prior written permission of the Publisher, or authorization through payment of the appropriate per-copy fee to the Copyright Clearance Center, Inc., 222 Rosewood Drive, Danvers, MA 01923, (978) 750-8400, fax (978) 750-4470, or on the web at www.copyright.com. Requests to the Publisher for permission should be addressed to the Permissions Department, John Wiley & Sons, Inc., 111 River Street, Hoboken, NJ 07030, (201) 748-6011, fax (201) 748-6008, or online at http://www.wiley.com/go/permission.

Trademarks: Wiley and the Wiley logo are trademarks or registered trademarks of John Wiley & Sons, Inc. and/or its affiliates in the United States and other countries and may not be used without written permission. All other trademarks are the property of their respective owners. John Wiley & Sons, Inc. is not associated with any product or vendor mentioned in this book.

Limit of Liability/Disclaimer of Warranty: While the publisher and author have used their best efforts in preparing this book, they make no representations or warranties with respect to the accuracy or completeness of the contents of this book and specifically disclaim any implied warranties of merchantability or fitness for a particular purpose. No warranty may be created or extended by sales representatives or written sales materials. The advice and strategies contained herein may not be suitable for your situation. You should consult with a professional where appropriate. Further, readers should be aware that websites listed in this work may have changed or disappeared between when this work was written and when it is read. Neither the publisher nor authors shall be liable for any loss of profit or any other commercial damages, including but not limited to special, incidental, consequential, or other damages.

For general information on our other products and services, please contact our Customer Care Department within the United States at (800) 762-2974, outside the United States at (317) 572-3993. For product technical support, you can find answers to frequently asked questions or reach us via live chat at https://support.wiley.com.

If you believe you've found a mistake in this book, please bring it to our attention by emailing our reader support team at wileysupport@wiley.com with the subject line "Possible Book Errata Submission."

Wiley also publishes its books in a variety of electronic formats. Some content that appears in print may not be available in electronic formats. For more information about Wiley products, visit our web site at www.wiley.com.

Library of Congress Cataloging-in-Publication Data is Available:

ISBN 9781394312108 (Paperback)
ISBN 9781394312122 (ePub)
ISBN 9781394312146 (ePDF)

Cover Design: Wiley
Cover Images: © Marharyta/stock.adobe.com
Author Photo: Courtesy of the Author

*To all of the students who are called "bad," "difficult,"
or "impossible," you deserve the world. For all the teachers who are told,
"you're not doing enough." This book is for you.*

Contents

Introduction		ix
CHAPTER 1	Eloping	1
CHAPTER 2	Back Talk	17
CHAPTER 3	School Refusal	37
CHAPTER 4	Helplessness	59
CHAPTER 5	Disruptive Behavior	81
CHAPTER 6	Anxiety	105
CHAPTER 7	Aggression	133
CHAPTER 8	Inattention	157
CHAPTER 9	Dishonesty	181
CHAPTER 10	Bullying	203
CHAPTER 11	The Elephant in the Room	225

Acknowledgments	233
About the Author	235
References	237
Index	239

Introduction

Let's face it: Teaching is not for the faint of heart. There's a unique kind of exhaustion that comes with being both an educator and a classroom manager. As a seasoned educator myself, I am not here to sugar coat our profession. Some days, you feel like you're juggling a dozen roles at once—mentor, mediator, counselor, and, yes, sometimes even referee. Between lesson planning, grading, and building meaningful connections with your students, navigating the endless stream of behavioral challenges can feel overwhelming. The outbursts, disruptions, and conflicts? They're just the cherry on top of an already full plate.

You're not alone in this. And guess what? There's no such thing as a perfect classroom. Managing challenging behaviors isn't about being a perfect teacher—it's about having the right tools, strategies, and mindset to support your students while keeping your own well-being intact. This book was created as a practical guide for educators who find themselves managing difficult behaviors daily.

Throughout this book, we'll dive into 10 specific types of challenging behavior that are all too common in classrooms. Each chapter will break down one behavior, explore the possible triggers and root causes, and—most importantly—give you tangible strategies for addressing it. Each chapter has two case studies of seeing these behaviors and their strategies in action. The idea is to help you better understand why these behaviors happen and offer some go-to methods to create a classroom that feels manageable and positive for both you and your students.

And because we know that handling challenging behaviors can take a serious toll on your mental and emotional health, we're ending the book with a final chapter that's all about you. We'll talk about self-care, setting boundaries, and finding ways to recharge because you are a person, not a superhero, and we all need space at the end of the day.

Why Challenging Behaviors Happen

Before we dive into each specific behavior, let's take a step back and look at the bigger picture. Why do challenging behaviors happen? Often, what we see as "bad" behavior is really just a way for students to communicate something they might not have the words for. Dr. Lori Desautels, an expert in educational neuroscience, talks about how behaviors are a form of communication. I know we have all heard this statement a time or two, but when we actually sit in it for a minute to consider what it really means, it's incredibly powerful. When a student is acting out, it's not just about defiance or disruption—it's their way of saying, "Hey, something isn't right here."

Dr. Bruce Perry, a leading voice in childhood trauma, emphasizes that many behaviors are actually rooted in a dysregulated nervous system. For students who've experienced trauma or chronic stress, their brains might be in survival mode, which makes them hypervigilant, impulsive, or prone to outbursts. They're not trying to be difficult; their brains are just currently wired to respond to stress in ways that can make learning really tough.

And then there's anxiety, something we're seeing more and more in students of all ages. Dr. Marc Brackett, from the Yale Center for Emotional Intelligence, highlights the fact that emotions drive behavior, and when anxiety takes over, it can manifest as avoidance, aggression, or even perfectionism. Sometimes, the kids who seem to be the most challenging are the ones who are struggling the most internally.

What You'll Find in Each Chapter

Each chapter in this book will tackle one specific behavior. These behaviors might look a little different from one student to the next, and there's no one-size-fits-all solution. But by understanding the causes and having a range of strategies to try, you'll be better equipped to support your students without losing your mind in the process.

Here's a peek into the next chapters:

Eloping (Running Away)

Few things are as stressful as a student running out of the classroom or even off school grounds. In this chapter, we'll talk about why eloping happens and how to create a classroom environment that minimizes the triggers for students who bolt when they feel overwhelmed. We'll also explore how to keep your students safe while building trust with the ones who are most likely to flee.

Back Talk

It's not just about sass (though sometimes it feels that way). When students talk back, there's usually something deeper going on—whether it's a need for autonomy or a struggle with authority. We'll look at strategies to de-escalate these power struggles, give students the control they need, and still keep your classroom running smoothly.

School Refusal

This is a big one. When a student simply refuses to come to school, it can be a nightmare for teachers and parents alike. In this chapter, we'll break down what might be causing school refusal and how to work with the student, their family, and the school team to get them back into the classroom—one step at a time.

Helplessness

Ever had a student who gives up before they even start? Helplessness can be incredibly frustrating to deal with because no amount of encouragement seems to help. We'll explore ways to re-engage these students, build their confidence, and help them develop the skills they need to succeed—without becoming too reliant on adult help.

Disruptive Behavior

Disruptions can take all kinds of forms—talking out of turn, making noises, distracting others—but the result is the same: The whole class gets thrown off. We'll dive into the root causes of disruptive behavior and talk about how to create a classroom that keeps students engaged and focused, minimizing the need for constant redirection.

Anxiety

Anxiety doesn't always show up the way you might expect. Sometimes, it looks like perfectionism and other times like avoidance or even outbursts. In this chapter, we'll look at how anxiety affects students' ability to learn and participate, and we'll talk about simple, effective strategies to help students manage their anxiety in the classroom.

Aggression

Dealing with aggression—whether it's physical or verbal—is tough for everyone involved. We'll explore why aggression happens, how to de-escalate situations before they get out of hand, and how to teach students safer and healthier ways to express their frustration and anger.

Inattention

Whether it's caused by ADHD, anxiety, or something else, inattention can seriously impact a student's ability to learn. We'll talk about ways to structure your classroom to support focus, provide appropriate sensory outlets, and help students develop their self-regulation skills.

Dishonesty

Lying can be a tricky behavior to address because it's often a defense mechanism. In this chapter, we'll talk about why students might resort to dishonesty and how to create an environment that encourages honesty, accountability, and trust.

Bullying

Bullying is a beast that takes many forms—physical aggression, social exclusion, online harassment—and it can have devastating effects on both the victim and the perpetrator. We'll explore strategies for addressing bullying in your classroom while fostering a culture of kindness, inclusion, and mutual respect.

The Final Chapter: The Elephant in the Room

I know more than most that managing challenging behavior day in and day out can leave you feeling completely drained. That's why the last chapter in this book is dedicated to you, the teacher. We'll explore how to take care of yourself while navigating the ups and downs of classroom behavior. Kristin Souers and Pete Hall, who work extensively in fostering resilient learners, remind us that self-care isn't a luxury; it's a necessity. When you're taking care of your mental, emotional, and physical health, you're better able to show up for your students.

We'll dive into practical strategies for managing stress, finding balance, and setting boundaries. We'll talk about vicarious trauma, tapping into your support network, and building routines that help you recharge—because when you're at your best, your students benefit, too.

Wait, Who are You?

Before I get too in the weeds here, I should introduce myself. My name is Allie Szczecinski. I'm Polish by association, hence the intense amount of consonants together in my surname. (Fun fact, Szczecin is a beautiful city in Poland, so my last name means "of Szczecin" in the Polish language!) I am the daughter of a special educator as my mom taught children with disabilities for decades here in Illinois. I grew up fascinated by her work and found myself always championing my peers with disabilities in school. It was a surprise to no one when I began my freshman year at Illinois State University as a special education major and never looked back. Over the years, I have taught in huge urban districts, suburban schools, and residential treatment facilities. From supporting children in self-contained settings with limited verbal abilities, AAC devices, and alternate curriculums to emotional behavior disorders and getting a crash course in the foster care system, I haven't quite seen it ALL, but I've seen a lot. I have worked with teachers in schools with extremely limited resources and also in schools with some of the highest property taxes in the nation. I have found that regardless of where you teach, children of all levels of need will be found at your school. All children deserve high-quality, excellent teachers, and all teachers deserve to have access to the right tools to be that kind of professional for children without sacrificing their own well-being.

Why This Book Matters

So, why another book on behavior management? Because classrooms are ever-evolving and so are the challenges we face as educators. Each student is different, each behavior is different, and the solutions that work for one class might not work for the next. This book isn't about turning you into a perfect teacher with perfect students—because that's just not realistic, and it doesn't exist. It's about giving you practical, research-based strategies that you can implement right away, helping you navigate the daily challenges of teaching while keeping your own well-being in mind.

As you read through this book, remember to give yourself some grace. No one has all the answers, and teaching is a constant process of learning, adapting, and growing. But with a proactive mindset, a compassionate heart, and a well-stocked toolbox of strategies, you can create a classroom environment where both you and your students can thrive.

Let's tackle these tricky behaviors together so we can stop saying we're always "teacher tired." We've got this!

CHAPTER ONE

Eloping

Understanding and Addressing Student Elopement

Ah, student elopement. No, I don't mean secretly getting married—though that sounds intriguing! I mean students who run away—from the area, from the setting, from the classroom, from the building. It's one of those behaviors we generally cannot ignore and is incredibly disruptive to student learning.

And yeah, language matters. I'm not trying to sound lofty or important by calling fleeing "elopement." I call it this because it's a more respectful way to discuss this behavior. After all, that's what it is, a behavior students exhibit. I also refrain from calling a student "a runner." I hear so many educational teams using this term to describe children, and it's an unfortunate label that doesn't sit well with me. So what do I say instead? "A student who tends to elope when _____." Did you catch what I did there? "A student who tends to elope when _____." That when? That's the secret sauce.

Why Language Matters

Labeling students can create fixed mindsets not only in educators but also in the students themselves. Dr. Marc Brackett, director of the Yale Center for Emotional Intelligence, stresses the importance of labeling emotions and behaviors in ways that don't pigeonhole students. When a child is labeled "a runner," the focus is placed on a behavior rather than the underlying cause. Labeling a student in this way can also affect how other teachers and students perceive the child. It becomes the defining feature of their identity within the school setting, leading to an over-simplified understanding of complex behavioral challenges.

Instead, describing a student's behavior in terms of triggers—like "a student who tends to elope when overwhelmed or anxious"—keeps the focus on the root cause and opens the door for solutions. It humanizes the behavior and reminds us that elopement is often a signal that a student's emotional needs are not being met. This is an important distinction because how we talk about behavior can shape how we address it.

Elopement: Not Just Running, But Escaping

While it may seem that a behavior like eloping can often come out of left field, there is always a reason why a student is running away from an area. Sometimes, the "why" is obvious—perhaps the child is overwhelmed by a difficult task, experiencing sensory overload, or reacting to a peer conflict. Other times, the root cause can feel trickier to pinpoint, but it's there. Elopement is an attempt to escape something, whether it's an overwhelming feeling, a stressful situation, or an unmet need.

Dr. Lori Desautels, an expert in educational neuroscience, emphasizes that behaviors like elopement are often a student's attempt to regulate overwhelming and uncomfortable emotions. According to her, when students flee, they are not being defiant but are experiencing a neurological response to stress or anxiety. This perspective helps educators reframe their approach, seeing elopement as a cry for help rather than mere misbehavior. By acknowledging the brain's role in behavior, educators can design interventions that address the underlying needs of students, like providing a sense of safety and control.

Understanding Elopement and Emotional Regulation

To gain a deeper understanding of elopement, it's crucial to delve into the concept of emotional regulation. Dr. Bruce Perry, a leading expert on childhood trauma, highlights that students who exhibit elopement behaviors often have difficulty regulating their emotions. These students may have heightened stress responses that are triggered by factors that seem minor to others but are deeply overwhelming to them.

For example, students might elope when they are asked to participate in a group activity because the social dynamics of group work trigger feelings of anxiety. Other students might elope during a noisy transition between subjects because the sensory overload is too much for them to handle. Understanding these triggers is key to addressing elopement behavior.

Dr. Marc Brackett suggests that creating emotionally supportive environments can significantly reduce challenging behaviors like elopement. He emphasizes the importance of teaching students emotional regulation skills, enabling them to articulate their feelings rather than resorting to elopement. Schools that integrate emotional intelligence into their curricula see improvements in student behavior, including a reduction in elopement incidents. His work highlights the importance of fostering emotional awareness and regulation in students as a proactive strategy to prevent elopement from happening.

Proactive Strategies to Address Elopement

Here are three proactive strategies educators can utilize to address student elopement:

Replace the Behavior

Providing a replacement behavior is the most essential intervention for children that's eloping from the classroom. We need to figure out what is causing children to leave and find a safer, more effective way for them to meet that same need.

Dr. Ross Greene, author of *The Explosive Child*, suggests that understanding the student's unmet needs is crucial for effective behavior intervention. If students are eloping because they are trying to escape work demands, an effective replacement behavior would allow them to exit the work in a structured way. This might look like giving children a break card system or creating a designated calm corner where they can retreat without physically leaving the classroom.

For example, if students feel overwhelmed during math, instead of fleeing, they could be taught to hand the teacher a break card, signaling that they need five minutes in a calm corner. This intervention allows children to achieve the same goal—escaping the situation—but in a safer, more constructive way. Even if children spend a significant amount of time in the calm corner initially, it's far safer and more ideal than escaping the classroom altogether. Over time, the goal is to gradually reintroduce children to the task as they develop coping mechanisms and emotional regulation skills.

Provide and Embed Choices

We need to face it: No matter how much play and creativity are involved in childhood, it can feel incredibly hard to be a kid. Students are constantly being told what to do, how to do it, and when to do it. For some students, this lack of autonomy can be overwhelming, leading them to escape situations where they feel powerless.

Offering controlled choices throughout the day can give students an element of control and meaningful independence. Having even a small "say" in how the day unfolds can be transformative for a student's mindset. Dr. Desautels suggests that offering students choices helps them feel empowered and reduces the likelihood of escape behaviors. When students feel more in control of their day, they are less likely to engage in elopement.

For example, you might offer students the choice of which activity to complete first, what type of writing utensil to use, or where to sit during independent work time. While it may seem trivial to us, these small choices give students a sense of agency, making it less likely that they will feel the need to flee from a situation where they perceive they have no control.

Structure the Day—with Student Input

Some of the most insightful information regarding student behavior comes straight from the students themselves. When setting up the day, it's important that students—especially those who are prone to eloping—know the schedule for the day and can see it visually.

Dr. Brackett emphasizes the importance of predictability in helping students manage their emotions. Having a written schedule helps ground students, giving their nervous system something to rely on. For students prone to elopement, knowing when a break is coming up can help them stay focused, knowing they'll get a break soon. For example, if students can see that in 30 minutes there's a brain break, they may be able to push through the current task.

Allowing students to have input in the schedule can also be powerful. For example, you might ask students, "Where in our schedule do you think you might need a brain break today?" Giving students this voice not only helps them develop self-awareness but also helps them feel a sense of ownership over their day.

What Happens When Students Elope? What Do I Do?

One of the most common and nerve-wracking questions educators ask about elopement is, "What do I do when a child bolts from the classroom?" It's a question that doesn't have one easy answer because elopement situations vary so much depending on the student, the school's protocols, and the context.

Dr. Desautels emphasizes that remaining calm and avoiding escalating the situation is critical. Chasing students can sometimes escalate their anxiety or encourage the behavior if they are seeking attention. However, we also have a duty to ensure the safety of the student and others.

Here are a few steps to consider when a student elopes:

1. **Ensure the Safety of the Other Students:** If you are the only adult in the room, ensure that the other students are safe and supervised. You might assign a trusted student as a peer leader while you briefly follow the eloping student or use a walkie-talkie to communicate with school support staff for immediate help.

2. **Avoid Engaging in a Chase:** Chasing students can heighten their stress response or turn the situation into a game. Instead, try walking at a calm, steady pace and using a gentle, non-threatening voice to remind them that they are safe and that you are there to help them.

3. **Communicate with Support Staff:** Know your school's protocols for handling elopement. Many schools require teachers to alert the principal, counselor, or another staff member when a child elopes. This ensures that the situation is monitored and the necessary precautions are taken to ensure the student's safety.

4. **Follow the Student's IEP or Behavior Plan:** If the student has a behavior plan or IEP that addresses elopement, follow the steps outlined in

the plan. This might involve offering the student a break in a designated area or contacting a specific staff member for assistance.

The Role of Relationships in Preventing Elopement

A key element that cannot be overlooked in managing elopement is the relationship between the teacher and the student. Dr. Ross Greene emphasizes that strong relationships can serve as a protective factor against behaviors like elopement. When students feel understood and connected to their teachers, they are more likely to seek help rather than flee when they're overwhelmed.

As a former special education teacher, I know firsthand the anxiety that comes with a student leaving the classroom. It often feels like a failure—that somehow your relationship with those children wasn't strong enough to keep them within the classroom walls. However, building strong relationships is a process that takes time. Regular, intentional check-ins with the students and making space for them to express their feelings are critical in building trust and preventing future elopement.

A Collaborative Approach

Elopement is a complex behavior that requires a multifaceted approach. It's not just about keeping students physically safe but also emotionally secure. By understanding the emotional and neurological roots of elopement, providing proactive strategies, and working collaboratively with the entire school team, we can support students in managing their feelings and behaviors more effectively. Remember, elopement is not a failure—it's an opportunity to understand our students on a deeper level and provide them with the support they need to thrive.

Case Study #1

Ethan is a 10-year-old 5th-grade student at Meadowbrook Elementary School. Known for his curiosity and creativity, Ethan excels in hands-on subjects like science and art. Ethan received Multi-Tiered System of Supports (MTSS) services for behavior and was in a few behavioral skill groups from K-3 grade. His behavior always improved with Tier 2 interventions, and he never needed more intensive support. However, teachers since kindergarten have noted that Ethan has always struggled with emotional regulation, particularly when faced with overwhelming stimuli or challenging tasks. He perceives reading as very challenging and often appears highly triggered by making mistakes. This often leads to a concerning behavior: elopement. When Ethan feels overwhelmed, he leaves the classroom without permission, seeking refuge in quieter areas of the school, such as the library. When the weather is clear, Ethan has been known to run out the back door of the school and hide underneath parts of the school playground.

About MTSS

The Multi-Tiered System of Supports (MTSS) is a comprehensive framework designed to address the academic, behavioral, and social emotional needs of all students through a tiered approach. It provides a structure for educators to deliver support at varying levels of intensity based on student needs.

Tier 1 focuses on high-quality, universal instruction and proactive strategies that benefit every student. For students needing additional assistance, Tier 2 offers targeted interventions in small groups, while Tier 3 delivers intensive, individualized support.

The MTSS emphasizes data-driven decision making, collaboration, and continuous monitoring to ensure that all students receives the right level of support for their success at school.

Identifying the Problem

Ethan's elopement poses fairly significant safety risks and disrupts both his learning and that of his peers. His elopement began when new reading centers were introduced toward the end of his 4th grade year. Since starting 5th grade, Ethan eloped 6 times in 2 weeks. The school staff, including his teacher, Ms. Johnson, the school counselor, Mr. Lee, and the principal, Ms. Garcia, recognized the need for a proactive approach to address Ethan's elopement.

Initial Observations

Ms. Johnson noted that Ethan's elopement typically occurred during reading tasks, including word problems in math, literacy tasks, and during classroom book clubs. The behavior seemed to be an escape mechanism, allowing him to avoid uncomfortable emotions when reading became challenging. It also seemed as though Ethan was especially overwhelmed when peers witnessed a mistake he made while reading.

Problem-Solving Approach

The school's problem-solving team decided on a multi-faceted approach to help Ethan manage his emotions and reduce elopement incidents. This plan included creating a supportive classroom environment, teaching coping strategies, and establishing a personalized intervention in the form of a classroom calm corner.

Team Collaboration

1. **Ms. Johnson (5th grade teacher):** Focused on classroom strategies and implementing the calm corner.
2. **Mr. Lee (School Counselor):** Worked with Ethan on emotional regulation and coping skills.
3. **Ms. Garcia (Principal):** Provided administrative support and ensured school-wide safety protocols were in place.

Creating the Calm Corner

The calm corner was designed to be a welcoming space for all students, promoting emotional regulation and offering a break from classroom stressors. However, it included personalized elements tailored to Ethan's needs.

Design and Features
- **Location:** A quiet corner of the classroom away from high-traffic areas.
- **Seating:** A comfortable bean bag chair and soft cushions.
- **Visuals:** Posters with calming strategies that Ethan was pre-taught by Mr. Lee, such as deep breathing exercises and positive affirmations.
- **Tools:** A set of noise-canceling headphones, a visual timer, stress balls, and fidget toys.
- **Personalized Items for Ethan:**
    - A small journal for writing or drawing his feelings.
    - A photo album with pictures of his family and pets.
    - A playlist of calming music he can listen to with headphones.

Implementing the Intervention

With the calm corner ready, the team introduced the concept to Ethan and the entire class. The goal was to normalize the use of the calm corner as a tool for anyone feeling overwhelmed, thus reducing any stigma associated with its use.

Educating the Class

Ms. Johnson held a class meeting to introduce the calm corner. She explained that everyone experiences stress and emotions in different ways, and having a dedicated space to manage those feelings is important. The class discussed how they might use the calm corner, and Ms. Johnson encouraged students to share their thoughts and ideas.

Across the introductory week, all students had an opportunity to explore the calm corner for 5 minutes each while adhering to the expectations for the calm corner that the class developed together.

Personalized Plan for Ethan

Mr. Lee worked with Ethan to develop a personalized plan for utilizing the calm corner. They created a signal that Ethan could use to indicate when he needed to use the calm corner. This nonverbal cue helped Ethan communicate his needs without disrupting the class. The cue also allowed for Ms. Johnson to see that Ethan was experiencing high stress, and that when she was available, he'd like her to check in with him. Ethan expressed that it helped when Ms. Johnson was able to support him when he was overwhelmed. This personalized plan acted as the replacement behavior, and this was explained to Ethan.

Monitoring Progress

The team closely monitored Ethan's use of the calm corner and overall behavior for 4 weeks. They met weekly during this time to discuss observations and make any necessary adjustments to the intervention.

Initial Challenges

Initially, Ethan was hesitant to use the calm corner. He shared with Mr. Lee that he feared it might draw attention to his struggles. To address this, Ms. Johnson discreetly encouraged its use and modeled the behavior by using the corner herself when feeling stressed. She also publicly suggested it to students regularly who were frustrated by assignments or feeling really energetic after recess or physical education (PE) class, as well as reminding students of it before starting tricky tasks.

Positive Developments

Over time, Ethan began to use the calm corner more frequently. He reported feeling more in control of his emotions and liked having a designated space to regroup. His instances of elopement decreased significantly, and he started to articulate his feelings more effectively after having space and time to decompress and regulate.

Adjustments and Future Steps

Based on data collection and talking to Ethan for anecdotal evidence, the team identified areas for further improvement and expansion.

Continuous Support for Ethan

- **Ongoing Counseling:** Mr. Lee slotted Ethan into an existing skills group related to coping skills and emotional regulation.
- **Increased Independence:** The team encouraged Ethan to suggest additional personal items or strategies for the calm corner, to help foster a sense of ownership and build his self-management and self awareness skills.
- **Reading Intervention:** The team took careful time to review Ethan's reading scores to ensure nothing was missed in his performance. While his reading scores fall into the average range, it was noted that he should continue to be monitored regularly to ensure that his emotional struggles aren't related to a deficit in reading that should be supported.

The case study of Ethan highlights the effectiveness of a targeted, personalized approach in addressing challenging behaviors like elopement. It shows that interventions rarely work instantaneously, and that giving time to interventions and replacement behaviors can allow for success. Creating a proactive intervention that actually impacted ALL students positively allowed for an increase in Tier 1 supports for Ms. Johnson's class, as well as meeting the intense needs of one student.

Case Study #2

Sophia is a 7-year-old second-grade student at Lincoln Elementary School. She is known for her vibrant personality and creativity, particularly in art and storytelling. Sophia is new to Lincoln Elementary for second grade and came in with limited paperwork from her previous school out of state. Sophia's teacher has identified that she has difficulty managing her emotions during social disagreements with peers. When conflicts arise, whether large or small, she often feels overwhelmed and resorts to eloping from the classroom and hiding in lockers or bathroom stalls.

Sophia's elopement behavior is concerning because it poses safety risks and disrupts her learning and that of her classmates. The school staff, including her teacher, Mrs. Thompson, the school counselor, Ms. Mika, and the principal, Ms. Livingston, recognized the need for a comprehensive approach to address Sophia's elopement.

Initial Observations

Mrs. Thompson observed that Sophia's elopement usually occurred during more unstructured times, such as group activities and projects or classroom free choice time. The elopement seemed to be an escape mechanism, allowing her to avoid social conflict and emotional discomfort.

Problem-Solving Approach

The school's problem-solving team decided that the increase in Sophia's incident reports due to eloping qualified her to join an MTSS Tier 2 social group with Ms. Mika, the school counselor. This group targets coping skills and social problem-solving skills. Additionally, Mrs. Thompson would focus on classroom-wide strategies that can support all students while reinforcing skills taught in the Tier 2 social group with Ms. Mika.

Team Collaboration

1. **Mrs. Thompson (Teacher):** Focused on classroom strategies and implementing the interventions and skills taught in social group.
2. **Ms. Mika (School Counselor):** Worked with Sophia in a Tier 2 social group on emotional regulation and social problem-solving skills.
3. **Ms. Livingston (Principal):** Provided administrative support and ensured school-wide safety protocols were in place.

Designing the Intervention

The team developed a targeted intervention plan to address Sophia's needs, focusing on teaching replacement behaviors and providing her with tools to manage conflicts safely and as independently as possible.

Components of the Intervention

1. **MTSS Social Group:**
   - Ms. Mika conducted weekly sessions with Sophia and other 2nd-grade peers to teach social problem-solving skills and emotional regulation techniques within a small group setting. They practiced scenarios where peers could express their feelings using "I" statements and seek help from an adult when needed.

2. **Calm Corner:**
   - Mrs. Thompson revitalized the calm corner in the classroom as a safe space for Sophia and her classmates to use when feeling overwhelmed.
   - The corner became more than just a break space and was now filled with calming tools like stress balls, a weighted blanket, and noise-canceling headphones. Mrs. Thompson introduced a new calming tool each morning during Morning Meeting and had each student try the tool out before putting it in the calm corner.

3. **Replacement Behavior:**
   - Sophia was taught to use a "peace card," which she could give to Mrs. Thompson or Ms. Mika when she needed a break from a social situation.
   - The peace card allowed Sophia to take a short break in the calm corner instead of eloping from the classroom.

4. **Peer Support:**
   - Mrs. Thompson facilitated class discussions about empathy, kindness, and conflict resolution to foster a supportive classroom environment.

- Sophia was paired with a "buddy" who could help her navigate social situations and provide support during group activities.

Implementing the Intervention

The intervention was introduced to Sophia and the entire class to normalize its use and reduce any stigma associated with seeking help.

Educating the Class

Mrs. Thompson used Morning Meeting and Closing Circle, two already existing parts of the class's daily schedule, to introduce the new and improved calm corner and the peace card with the class. She explained that everyone experiences emotions and social situations differently, and it's okay, and responsible, to seek help when needed. The class discussed how they might use the calm corner and shared ideas for supporting each other.

Personalized Plan for Sophia

Ms. Mika worked with Sophia to develop a personalized plan. They practiced using the peace card and role-played different scenarios to help Sophia feel comfortable with the new strategies.

Monitoring Progress

The team closely monitored Sophia's use of the intervention and her overall behavior. They met weekly to discuss observations and make any necessary adjustments.

Initial Challenges

Initially, Sophia was hesitant to use the peace card and calm corner. She struggled to identify when would be an appropriate time to use either. To address this, Mrs. Thompson discreetly encouraged its use and praised Sophia for taking proactive steps to manage her emotions. She utilized positive phone calls home every time Sophia used a strategy with support or independently.

Positive Developments

Over time, Sophia began to use the peace card more frequently. She reported feeling more in control of her emotions and liked having the calm corner to regulate rather than hide in a locker or the bathroom. Over the first month, instances of elopement decreased significantly.

Adjustments and Future Steps

Based on data collection and talking to Sophia for anecdotal evidence, the team identified areas for further improvement and expansion.

Continuous Support for Sophia

- **Ongoing Counseling:** Ms. Mika continued to meet with Sophia in the Tier 2 group. To encourage progress, she enrolled Sophia in the group for a second round.
- **Increased Independence:** The team encouraged Sophia to teach some of the social problem-solving strategies from her group with the class.

Conclusion

The case study of Sophia highlights the effectiveness of a targeted, personalized approach in addressing elopement. By creating an intervention tailored to Sophia's needs, the school was able to provide her with the tools to manage her emotions constructively. The intervention already existed as a component of the school-wide MTSS plan. This Tier 2 intervention helped to not only reduce elopement incidents but also contributed to a more inclusive and empathetic classroom environment. Through collaboration and creativity, the school fostered a supportive space where Sophia and her peers could thrive both academically *and* socially.

CHAPTER TWO

Back Talk

ALL BEHAVIOR is communication. We hear this a lot, and it's true—every action students take is a way for them to express their feelings, needs, or struggles. However, simply understanding this important fact about behavior really isn't enough. Recognizing that behavior is communication doesn't magically equip us with the tools or skills necessary to support students through tough moments. When we face student defiance, it's challenging not only for us as educators but also for the students themselves.

Understanding Behavior as Communication

According to Dr. Lori Desautels, behaviors such as back talk or defiance are often expressions of unmet needs or emotional dysregulation. She emphasizes the importance of recognizing that these behaviors are actually signals from the student's brain that something is not right internally. For example, students who talk back might be communicating feelings of frustration, fear, or a need for autonomy that they cannot articulate in more socially acceptable ways. When we see defiant behavior as a form of communication rather than simple misbehavior, it allows us to get curious about what's going on beneath the surface.

Dr. Marc Brackett, director of the Yale Center for Emotional Intelligence, suggests that the key to addressing defiant behavior is to approach it with empathy and curiosity rather than punishment. When we stop seeing back talk as black-and-white "rude" behavior and start examining the behavior with a curious mindset, we can uncover the underlying issues and actually make moves toward resolving them. For instance, a student who consistently engages in back talk might be struggling with anxiety about schoolwork or experiencing overwhelming stress from situations at home or with peers.

Let's say students snap, "Why do I have to do this?" every time they're asked to start a challenging assignment. It might feel like disrespect, but those students could be expressing frustration and fear of failure, emotions that are hard to name in the moment. Brackett would recommend shifting our approach to one of understanding: Instead of shutting down the back talk with a reprimand, engage the students in a conversation. Ask open-ended questions like, "What's feeling tough about this right now?" You'd be surprised how much you can discover just by taking that empathetic pause.

Building a Toolbox for Support

Addressing back talk effectively requires a robust toolbox of strategies and skills. Dr. Ross Greene, known for his work on collaborative problem solving, advocates for involving students in the process of finding solutions to their behavioral challenges. Greene's approach emphasizes understanding the students' perspective and working together to develop strategies that address their needs. For example, if a student is frequently interrupting the class with back talk, the teacher might sit down with them to determine why they feel the need to speak out. Together, they can collaboratively develop a plan to manage their impulses more effectively.

Think about a student who is always pushing back during group work, insisting, "This is stupid. I'm not doing it." Instead of jumping to a consequence, Greene suggests having a problem-solving conversation. Ask the student, "What makes group work frustrating for you?" Perhaps the student feels ignored or overwhelmed in groups, and together, you can come up with strategies to make group activities more manageable—like giving he or she a specific role they enjoy or pairing them with a supportive peer. I also have to add—this is not easy to do. Oftentimes, our natural response to back talk is a defensive one. Give yourself a moment to take a deep breath, count to 10 in your head, and gather your thoughts before responding. This pause can give you the much needed reset before responding in a way that could very well start a power struggle.

Alex Shevrin Venet, an educator and advocate for trauma-informed practices, highlights the importance of creating a classroom environment where students feel safe and valued. She suggests that when students perceive their teachers as supportive and understanding, they are more likely to communicate their needs in constructive ways rather than through defiance. Practices like implementing restorative circles, where students can express their feelings and experiences in a safe and structured setting, help address and even prevent back talk. The practice of pausing before responding to students' snarky comments can also increase the safety students feel in the classroom. Strangely enough, boundaries and consistency from educators are often what kids are craving after all.

Let's say students snap at a peer during a group activity, and it escalates into back talk with the teacher. Instead of jumping straight to consequences, using a restorative practice—like holding a brief restorative conversation—allows the students to explain why they reacted that way. Maybe they felt unheard, or perhaps there was a misunderstanding. By giving students a chance to reflect and talk about the issue, we can de-escalate the situation and work together toward a solution.

Proactive Strategies and Examples

To effectively manage and respond to back talk, teachers can try these three proactive strategies:

Replace the Behavior

Providing a replacement behavior is one of the most effective and essential interventions for a child who is talking back. When addressing defiant behavior like back talk, the key is understanding the underlying cause and providing a more appropriate alternative behavior. As with elopement, identifying the root cause of the behavior is critical. We need to understand what is causing the child to talk back, followed by finding a more effective and respectful behavior that serves the same purpose as the back talk.

For example, students might talk back because they feel overwhelmed by a particular task. Instead of allowing the behavior to continue unchecked, we can teach the students how to use sentence stems to ask for help in a more respectful manner. Sentence stems like "I'm feeling frustrated because. . ." or "Can you help me with this part?" can empower the student to express their feelings without resorting to defiance.

Dr. Desautels emphasizes the importance of understanding the neurobiological and emotional triggers that might be causing students to engage in back talk. She suggests that behaviors like back talk often stem from unmet needs, like the need for autonomy, attention, or an escape from a difficult situation. Understanding these triggers helps us tailor interventions to meet the students' specific needs, like providing alternative ways to express their frustration or asking for help without interrupting the flow of the classroom.

For example, students who feel overwhelmed by the workload may use back talk to avoid completing tasks. By breaking down assignments into smaller, more manageable steps, you can reduce the students'

Examples of sentence stems, like the ones below, can be accessed using this QR code.

Respectful Talk

- I am frustrated because...
- Can you help me?
- I need space.
- My plan is...
- I am feeling ____ because ____.

frustration and provide them with a sense of accomplishment, reducing the need for back talk. You're meeting their need for success by adjusting the task itself rather than just addressing the defiant behavior.

Emotional Check-Ins

Incorporating regular emotional check-ins into your daily schedule is a simple yet essential practice for understanding and responding to your students' emotional needs. By gauging the emotional state of all students, teachers can proactively support those who might engage in back talk more frequently. This understanding allows teachers to create a learning environment that is responsive to students' needs, reducing the likelihood of disruptive behavior and enhancing overall classroom harmony.

Emotional check-ins can take many forms. Some teachers use tools like Dr. Brackett's mood meter, where students place their names or markers next to emotions listed on a chart. The mood meter gives students an accessible way to articulate how they're feeling, providing the teacher with immediate insight into the emotional climate of the room.

These check-ins can be especially helpful during transitions—those tricky times when emotions often run high. For example, after lunch or recess, students may feel more agitated or excitable. A simple emotional check-in at this point in the day can give the teacher valuable data about how students are feeling and allow for proactive adjustments. Maybe the teacher notices that several students are feeling anxious, so they decide to incorporate a brief mindfulness activity before moving into academic work. This small shift can prevent back talk or other disruptive behaviors before they begin.

In a recent example, a teacher implemented an emotional check-in system where students used a small journal to write or draw how they felt at the start of the day. One student who often engaged in back talk during math consistently reported feeling frustrated and anxious during these check-ins. The teacher used this information to offer the student additional math support and adjusted the way instructions were given. Over time, the student's defiant behavior decreased as he or she felt more equipped to manage their emotions and the challenges of the subject.

Dr. Desautels points out that emotional check-ins also strengthen teacher-student relationships. When students feel that their emotions are acknowledged and respected, they're more likely to feel secure and engaged in the classroom. This connection reduces anxiety and resistance, fostering a more supportive learning environment that naturally decreases back talk.

Think about key transition points in your day, and work to integrate emotional check-ins at these times. Consider adding check-ins before activities where back talk tends to occur. If you know that students struggle after recess, take five minutes to ask how everyone is feeling before jumping into the next lesson. This gives you the insight needed to adjust your approach and address potential issues proactively.

Restorative Practices

Restorative practices are both proactive and reactive strategies that can help address back talk and build a stronger classroom community. These practices focus on repairing harm, fostering empathy, and restoring relationships after conflict.

One simple restorative practice is the use of restorative conversations after an incident of back talk. For example, after students talk back during class, the teacher can pull them aside for a private conversation. This dialogue provides an opportunity for the student to express their feelings, understand the impact of their behavior, and explore ways to make amends.

During a restorative conversation, the teacher might ask the students, "What was going on for you when you said that?" This opens the door for the students to share their perspective and helps them feel heard. The teacher can then ask follow-up questions like, "How do you think your words affected the class?" and "What can we do to move forward?" This process helps the students reflect on their behavior, understand its impact, and take responsibility for their actions.

> "What was going on for you when you said that?"
> "How do you think your words affected the class?"
> "What can we do to move forward?"

Dr. Ross Greene emphasizes the importance of collaborative problem-solving during restorative conversations. He suggests that involving students in the process of finding solutions empowers them to take ownership of their behavior. This approach not only addresses the specific incident of back talk but also teaches valuable problem-solving and communication skills.

Another restorative practice is class discussions. Whether it's during a morning meeting, circle time, or advisory period, these group conversations allow students to share their experiences and feelings in a supportive environment. Class discussions can be used to proactively address issues like back talk by giving students space to discuss how they're feeling and reflect on how their actions impact others.

For example, a teacher might hold a circle time after noticing an increase in back talk during group work. The teacher can facilitate a discussion where students share how group work makes them feel and what they need to be successful. This practice helps build empathy and fosters a sense of belonging, reducing the need for students to use defiant behaviors to express their feelings.

Dr. Bruce Perry notes that restorative practices, such as apologies and reflection, help students understand the impact of their actions on others. Encouraging students to reflect on their behavior and, if appropriate, apologize to those affected, and teaches them accountability and empathy. While apologies should always come from the student's desire to make amends, offering space for reflection can help get to the root of back talk and strengthen relationships.

The Power of Proactive and Restorative Approaches

Addressing back talk and defiant behavior in the classroom requires a multi-faceted approach that emphasizes understanding, empathy, and collaboration. By recognizing that back talk is often a form of communication, we can shift from punitive responses to strategies that help students express their feelings in healthier ways.

Through replacement behaviors, emotional check-ins, and restorative practices, we can create classroom environments where students feel safe, supported, and empowered to communicate their needs constructively. In doing so, we reduce the occurrence of back talk and help students build the emotional regulation skills they need to thrive.

Ultimately, the key to managing back talk lies in creating a classroom culture where students feel heard, understood, and valued. When students know that their emotions matter and that they can express themselves without fear of punishment, they're far more likely to engage in positive behaviors and develop the social and emotional skills needed for success in and out of the classroom.

Case Study #1

Ella is an 8-year-old third-grade student at Pine Valley Elementary School. Ella is creative, competitive, and is very social. She often rushes through her schoolwork, resulting in numerous mistakes. Despite her potential, the quality of Ella's work suffers because of her tendency to prioritize speed over accuracy. When her teacher, Ms. Clark, provides feedback or asks her to slow down and review her work, Ella frequently responds with back talk, expressing frustration and defensiveness. Over time her back talk has increased in aggressiveness and has started to include swear words and a raised voice.

Ella's behavior has become a concern for both her academic progress and her relationship with her teacher and classmates. The school staff, including Ms. Clark, the school counselor, Mr. Parker, and the assistant principal, Mrs. Reynolds, decided to address Ella's behavior through a collaborative, structured approach that would help her develop more effective work habits and improve her communication skills.

Initial Observations

Ms. Clark observed that Ella consistently completed her assignments much faster than her peers. 5/5 times, Ella turned in her work by running to the finished bin and saying, "Done!" loudly. However, this speed came at the cost of accuracy—her work often contained numerous errors, and she missed key instructions. When Ms. Clark provided feedback, Ella tended to react with irritation, dismissive comments, or outright defiance, such as saying, "I did it fast because it's easy!" or "I don't care what you say, I am not doing it again!"

Problem-Solving Approach

It was clear to the team that Ella's behavior was beginning to affect her learning and the classroom dynamics. The problem-solving team at Pine Valley Elementary decided to develop a comprehensive intervention plan. This plan aimed to address both the root causes of Ella's rushing behavior and her tendency to respond to feedback with back talk.

Team Collaboration

1. **Ms. Clark (Teacher):** Focused on classroom strategies and implementing the intervention.
2. **Mr. Parker (School Counselor):** Helped build a simple and effective intervention and taught it privately to Ella.
3. **Mrs. Reynolds (Assistant Principal):** Provided administrative support and helped facilitate communication between school staff and Ella's parents.

Designing the Intervention

The team developed a multi-faceted intervention plan to help Ella develop more effective work habits and communication skills that would ideally support a lessen in back talk during the school day. The intervention was designed to be supportive, addressing both academic and emotional needs.

Components of the Intervention

1. **Work Quality Over Speed:**
    - **Setting Clear Expectations:** Ms. Clark began adding in "quality over speed" and examples of this expectation in her assignment directions. She emphasized this verbally and in written directives

before every assignment. Ms. Clark continually reminded all students of the importance of accuracy and thoroughness, explaining that careful work would be praised over quick work.

- **Checkpoints and Review:** Ella was given specific checkpoints during her work to pause and review her progress. These checkpoints helped her slow down and ensure that she was following instructions and minimizing mistakes.

2. **Respectful Communication:**

   - **Sentence Stems:** Ella still needed the ability to share her thoughts authentically, so the intervention aimed to provide more effective and respectful ways to do so. Ms. Clark introduced sentence stems that Ella could use when receiving feedback or any other time she felt frustrated by her teachers or peers. These included:

   - "I am frustrated because _____."
   - "I disagree because _____."
   - "Can you explain what I need to fix?"
   - "I didn't understand this part, could you help me with it?"

   - **Role-Playing:** Mr. Parker worked with Ella in a set of three direct counseling sessions to practice using these sentence stems. They role-played different scenarios where Ella might receive feedback or feel frustrated, helping her feel more comfortable and confident in responding respectfully.

3. **Parental Involvement:**

   - **Consistent Messaging:** Mrs. Reynolds facilitated regular communication between the school and Ella's parents, ensuring that they fully understood the reason behind the intervention as well as what it entailed. She delivered messages about the importance of quality work and respectful communication being consistent at home and school.

- **Home Reinforcement:** Ella's parents were given the same sentence stem visuals used by Ms. Clark and were encouraged to reinforce the use of sentence stems at home, particularly in situations where Ella felt frustrated or defensive.

Implementing the Intervention

With the intervention plan in place, Ms. Clark began implementing the new strategies in her classroom. The goal was to gradually shift Ella's focus from speed to accuracy and to help her develop healthier ways of responding to feedback and frustration.

Educating the Class

Ms. Clark introduced the concept of "Quality Over Speed" to the entire class. She explained that while finishing work quickly could be impressive, it was more important to take the time to do it well since class work was not designed to be a race. She reinforced this message by giving examples of how professionals—like artists, engineers, and doctors—must prioritize accuracy and thoroughness in their work. After the initial introduction of this concept, she reinforced this at the onset of every assignment the same way she would offer reminders about page numbers and writing their names on the top.

Personalized Support for Ella

Ella was initially resistant to the new expectations and the use of sentence stems. She felt frustrated by the emphasis on slowing down and was hesitant to use the new communication tools. To help her adjust, Ms. Clark provided gentle reminders and consistent positive reinforcement whenever Ella made even the smallest effort to follow the new plan. Ms. Clark also stayed in close contact with Ella's parents to provide positive feedback about every respectful communication exchange they had together.

Monitoring Progress

The team closely monitored Ella's progress, with regular check-ins to assess how well the intervention was working and to make any necessary adjustments.

Initial Challenges

At first, Ella struggled with the slower pace and the focus on accuracy. She continued to rush through her work though with slightly fewer mistakes and occasionally reverted to back talk when Ms. Clark reminded her of the plan. However, with consistent support and reinforcement, including a greater awareness of her classmate's pacing, Ella began to see the benefits of slowing down and taking her time.

Positive Developments

Over time, Ella started to come around to the new approach. She began to take pride in producing accurate work and earned recognition for her efforts, like having her work shown as an example for tricky math problems and being chosen to read her original poem at a school assembly. While she initially resisted using the sentence stems, Ella slowly began incorporating them into her interactions with Ms. Clark. This change helped to de-escalate situations that might have previously resulted in back talk.

Adjustments and Future Steps

Based on data collection, including Ella's work samples and grades as well as interviewing both Ella and Ms. Clark for anecdotal evidence, the team identified areas for further improvement and expansion.

Continuous Support for Ella

- **Ongoing Feedback:** Ms. Clark continued to provide structured feedback and encouragement to help Ella maintain her progress.

- **Advanced Sentence Stems:** As Ella became more comfortable with the initial sentence stems, she was introduced to more complex phrases that encouraged deeper reflection and self-assessment. Sentence stems were also included for interactions in PE class as suggested by Ella. Since she is very competitive by nature, Ella realized that she could benefit from some sentence stems to help during competitions in PE.

Conclusion

The case study of Ella highlights the importance of understanding the underlying causes of a student's behavior and implementing targeted, supportive interventions. By focusing on quality over speed and teaching respectful communication skills, the school was able to help Ella improve both her academic performance and her interactions with others. This case study also showed that the intervention brought Ella greater self awareness as she self requested sentence stems for interactions in PE class. The success of the intervention demonstrates how a thoughtful, collaborative approach can lead to meaningful and lasting changes in a student's behavior and learning outcomes. Through consistent support and reinforcement, Ella learned to value the quality of her work, and to express herself in more constructive and respectful ways.

Case Study #2

Ahmed is a 6-year-old first-grade student at Willow Creek Elementary School. He recently transferred to the school mid-year after being reunited with his mother following a period in foster care. His teacher, Ms. Johnson reports that Ahmed appears very bright and friendly, but his past school experiences were marked by frequent absences and attendance issues, making it difficult for her to accurately assess his academic levels.

Ahmed has made friends and is generally friendly, but he is often very moody. When Ahmed is in a good mood, he engages well with his peers and participates actively in class. However, there are days when he enters the class with a frown, scowling at Ms. Johnson and frequently engaging in back talk toward her. This can evolve into yelling, arguing, and other defiant behaviors. This has become a significant challenge in maintaining a positive and productive classroom environment and has changed the dynamic of the classroom since he enrolled.

Initial Observations

Ms. Johnson has observed that Ahmed's moods at times appear almost unpredictable, with his back talk often triggered by seemingly small events like a minor change in routine or having to use specific materials. Ms. Johnson has connected with Ahmed's mother, who shared that his current living and schooling situation is the most consistent it has ever been for him. Prior to this, he was used to moving frequently and not consistently attending school on time, or at all.

Problem-Solving Approach

Recognizing the need for a wrap-around approach to support Ahmed's emotional regulation, Ms. Johnson, along with the school counselor, Ms. Turner, and the school principal, Mr. Rodriguez, formed a problem-solving team to develop an intervention plan.

Team Collaboration

1. **Ms. Johnson (Teacher):** Focused on classroom strategies and implementing the intervention.
2. **Ms. Turner (School Counselor):** Worked with Ahmed on emotional regulation and better understanding his personal history.
3. **Mr. Rodriguez (Principal):** Provided administrative support, monitored attendance, and helped facilitate communication with Ahmed's mother.

Designing the Intervention

The team developed a multi-faceted intervention plan to address Ahmed's emotional regulation, attendance, and classroom behavior. The plan aimed to provide Ahmed with the structure and support needed to improve his mood stability and reduce instances of back talk.

Components of the Intervention

1. **Structured Emotional Check-Ins:**
   - **Daily Routine:** Ms. Johnson began implementing structured emotional check-ins during three key transition times of the day: morning arrival, after lunch, and before dismissal. These check-ins were designed to help not only Ahmed but also all of his classmates identify and share their feelings to support preparation for the upcoming activities.

2. **Replacement Behavior for Back Talk:**
   - **Calm-Down Strategies:** Ms. Turner introduced Ahmed to specific emotional regulation strategies, like deep breathing exercises, counting to 10, or using the already established "Calm Corner" in the classroom. These strategies were presented as alternatives to back talking when he felt upset or frustrated.
   - **Sentence Stems for Respectful Communication:** To help Ahmed communicate more respectfully, Ms. Johnson introduced sentence stems that he could use instead of yelling or arguing. These included phrases like:
     - "I'm feeling upset because _____."
     - "Can we talk about this later when I'm calmer?"
     - "I don't understand, can you help me?"
     - "I need space right now."

- **Role-Playing Scenarios:** Ahmed and Ms. Turner practiced these sentence stems during weekly counseling sessions through role-playing scenarios, helping Ahmed feel more comfortable using them in real situations.

Implementing the Intervention

With the intervention plan in place, Ms. Johnson began implementing the new strategies in her classroom. The goal was to create a more structured and supportive environment that would help Ahmed manage his emotions and reduce instances of back talk, while also using the same strategies to offer these skills and supports to all students.

Educating the Class

Ms. Johnson introduced the concept of emotional check-ins to the entire class by sharing that emotions matter, and that all emotions are valid. She showed the class a poster with 5 pictures of diverse children showing 5 different emotions through body language. Together, the class labeled each emotion. Ms. Johnson explained that all people have feelings that affect how they behave, and that it's important to name, understand, and talk about these feelings. She created a new icon for their classroom schedule that showed the three check-in times for the day. Students would use the poster to point to their current emotion and determine if they wanted to feel that way or if they were hoping to shift to a more comfortable emotion. The check-ins were presented as a normal part of the day, not just something for Ahmed, which helped normalize the practice and reduce any stigma.

Personalized Support for Ahmed

Ahmed was initially skeptical about both the emotional check-ins and the calm-down strategies. He found the check-ins to be "for babies" and resisted participating fully. Regardless of how he seemed to be feeling, he pointed to "mad" each time. However, Ms. Johnson persisted in making the check-ins engaging and relevant to Ahmed's interests. She noticed Ahmed's love of Sponge Bob and used pictures of this character showing the five emotions to make an alternative poster. Students could choose which one they wanted to use as their check-in poster at any point. Using the poster helped Ahmed begin using the check-ins more authentically, and he began making his own Sponge Bob emotions posters during free choice time.

Monitoring Progress

The team closely monitored Ahmed's progress, with regular check-ins to assess how well the intervention was working and to make any necessary adjustments.

Initial Challenges

At first, Ahmed's participation in the emotional check-ins was minimal, and he continued to struggle with back talking during moments of frustration or when he was in an uncomfortable mood. Without significant adult prompting, he was not using the calm corner or engaging in the regulation tools he was being taught and reinforced with the counselor.

Positive Developments

Over time, Ahmed started to participate more actively in the emotional check-ins, particularly when they included Sponge Bob. He began using the sentence stems introduced by Ms. Johnson and practiced with Ms. Turner, which helped him express his feelings more respectfully. When Ahmed checked in sharing he was sad, mad, or tired, Ms. Johnson could make accommodations to support his emotional needs.

Ahmed's attendance was 100% after moving to Willow Creek Elementary. His commitment to attending daily helped him build a meaningful relationship with his peers and teachers. Ahmed's attendance allowed for more consistent routines, which contributed to greater emotional stability and the ability to connect, trust, and engage with school in a meaningful way.

Adjustments and Future Steps

Based on the data collection and observations, the team identified areas for further improvement and considered expanding some of the strategies to benefit the entire class.

Continuous Support for Ahmed

- **Ongoing Emotional Support:** Ms. Johnson continued to provide structured emotional check-ins and tailored activities to help Ahmed manage his emotions and maintain positive behavior. He helped create emotion posters by using his blossoming art skills to make individual posters based on student interests.

Conclusion

The case study of Ahmed highlights the importance of understanding the student, his background, and allowing for relationships to form. By focusing on knowing the student, Ms. Johnson was able to press forward with the original intervention plan rather than scrap it when it felt as though it wasn't working. This case study also showed that relationships can truly be the catalyst for change. When the team learned that Ahmed had not experienced consistency in life prior to this season, they allowed him time to get comfortable with routines, relationships, and his new home and school environments. This proved to be especially meaningful. The success of the intervention demonstrates how an intentional, dynamic approach can lead to supportive tools for ALL students, not just one child who may be demonstrating challenging behavior.

CHAPTER THREE

School Refusal

IT'S EXHAUSTING, it's complicated, and it's overwhelming for all involved—school refusal. It's a behavior that challenges teachers, frustrates parents, and isolates students. The good news is that with the right strategies, we can support children who experience school refusal and make a real difference in their lives. Believe it or not, proactive strategies for this behavior are absolutely possible, and once they are in place, they can be transformative.

Understanding School Refusal

First, let's clarify what school refusal is—and what it isn't. It's not just students saying they don't want to go to school because they stayed up too late or didn't finish their homework. School refusal is a complex and ongoing behavior where children resist attending school due to underlying emotional or psychological reasons. These needs can range from anxiety, depression, bullying, learning difficulties, family issues, or even physical health problems (Heyne et al., 2011).

To understand school refusal, it's important to shift the focus from the behavior itself to the emotions driving it. Dr. Marc Brackett, director of the Yale Center for Emotional Intelligence, explains that understanding the emotional foundation of behaviors like school refusal is essential. Children may avoid school because they associate it with overwhelming feelings—fear of failure, social anxiety, or a sense of not belonging—and unless we identify and address these emotions, the issue persists. As educators, it's our job to dig deeper and find out why a student is resisting. Without understanding the "why," it's challenging, or dare I say close to impossible, to provide effective support.

Here's where school refusal can get tricky. It doesn't always start as full-blown avoidance. You may notice a student frequently tardy, taking longer to come inside after recess, or suddenly having "stomach aches" when math time rolls around. These can be signs of a student on the verge of school refusal. The sooner we recognize these signals, the quicker we can jump in with proactive strategies to curb the behavior before it escalates.

Building a Supportive Relationship

Our first step in addressing school refusal as teachers is to establish a supportive and empathetic relationship with the student. Dr. Lori Desautels emphasizes that "connection before correction" is key. Children who refuse school are often in a state of emotional dysregulation, and the last thing they need is to feel more pressure. Building a trusting relationship can help them feel safe enough to engage with school again.

Why is this so important? Think about it. If students feel like the teacher is only interested in their attendance or grades, it can increase their anxiety about school. But when a student knows that their teacher cares about them as a person and is willing to support them through difficult moments, it can make all the difference. Research shows that a trusting relationship with teachers can significantly reduce school refusal (Kearney & Graczyk, 2014). So, what do we do, and how does this start?

Warning Signs: What to Look For

While school refusal can show up unexpectedly, it's typically not surprising when a student begins to refuse school because there are usually warning signs. These signs could look like separation anxiety, appearing more detached, or not fully engaging in social relationships with peers. You may also start getting reports from home that getting to school is becoming increasingly difficult, or you may notice frequent tardiness.

This is where our proactive strategies really shine. By recognizing and addressing these behaviors early, we can intervene before they escalate. Let's talk about three strategies that can make a tremendous difference.

The 2 × 10 Strategy: Building Connection Through Small Moments

One powerful way to strengthen the teacher-student relationship and reduce school refusal is by using the 2 × 10 strategy, created by Dr. Raymond Wlodkowski. It's simple: For 10 consecutive days, spend two minutes each day having a personal conversation with a student who is exhibiting challenging behavior—such as a child at risk for school refusal. The key here is to talk about anything but schoolwork. The students want to talk about their new puppy, their favorite video game, or the cake they helped bake last night? Perfect! The goal is to build rapport and show genuine interest in the student as a person, not just as a student.

Research supports the effectiveness of this strategy in reducing negative behaviors and increasing student engagement. Dr. Wlodkowski's research found that when teachers consistently used the 2 × 10 strategy, problem behaviors decreased by as much as 85% (Wlodkowski, 1983). The success of this intervention lies in its simplicity—it's about showing the students you care about them beyond academics. This allows the children to feel seen and valued, which is often what they need the most.

For students showing signs of school refusal, this strategy can be a game-changer. By investing time in these brief, consistent interactions, teachers can create a stronger foundation of trust and respect that positively impacts the student's school experience. Sometimes, just knowing that someone will listen to them for a couple of minutes each day can shift students' perspectives on coming to school. Another perk? The adult involved in this intervention can create a simple log sheet to gather information about the personal interests of the students. This information can be offered up to other stakeholders (think related arts teachers, special education staff, or intervention teachers) to give them more insight into what this student might be interested in.

Collaborating with Stakeholders

Here's the truth: you can't and shouldn't do all of this by yourself. We teachers are notorious for piling too much on our plates, and school refusal is not a challenge you should tackle alone. Collaboration with other professionals in the school is absolutely crucial. School counselors, psychologists, and administrators play an essential role in supporting students through school refusal. Dr. Lori Desautels emphasizes the importance of leaning on others when handling complex behavior issues. A multidisciplinary approach is often the most effective way to address school refusal (Glad et al., 2013).

Here's how this works. You, as the teacher, are likely the first to notice signs of school refusal, but you don't have to be the only one managing it. Involving your school's mental health team can help you understand the root causes of the behavior and develop more comprehensive support. School counselors and psychologists can assess whether anxiety, depression, or trauma is playing a role and offer strategies that go beyond the

Try out this sample log sheet as a simple way to share this information as needed. To access, use the QR code below.

2X10 LOG

Student Name _____

Date	Chatted about...

classroom. They may recommend a formal or informal behavior intervention plan or suggest check-ins and related accommodations.

Don't forget the family in this process either. The family is the most consistent influence in the child's life, and research shows that strong family-school collaboration can have a hugely positive impact on overcoming school refusal (Kearney & Silverman, 1995). You may want to schedule a meeting with the family to learn about how things are going at home—how long has this been happening? Is the student expressing stress about specific parts of the day? The more information you have, the more individualized your approach can be.

Mindfulness and Coping Skills Education

We all know that students experience stress and anxiety. But how often do we give them the tools to manage those feelings? Dr. Desautels and other experts advocate for the use of mindfulness and coping strategies to help children manage anxiety and stress related to school refusal. The best part about teaching these strategies is that you can teach your entire class as a Tier 1 effort! This way, students who struggle with school refusal don't feel singled out, and everyone benefits from explicit social emotional lessons.

Start by incorporating simple mindfulness exercises like deep breathing, progressive muscle relaxation, or guided imagery. For instance, you could begin each morning with a few minutes of quiet breathing or introduce a "calm-down corner" where students can go to reset when they're feeling overwhelmed.

Another essential strategy is teaching positive self-talk. Have students brainstorm and practice positive affirmations that they can use when feeling anxious about school. This could be something like, "I can do hard things" or "It's okay to feel nervous." Practicing these affirmations can help students reframe negative thoughts and build resilience.

You can access a set of affirmation cards for students using the QR code below.

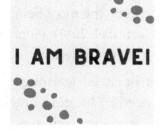

The beauty of these coping skills is that students can also use them outside of the classroom. You can share these strategies with parents so they can reinforce them at home, especially when the child is feeling anxious about going to school. The more we empower students with the tools to manage their feelings, the less school refusal will take hold.

When Proactive Strategies Aren't Enough: Reactive Strategies for School Refusal

Even with the best-laid plans, sometimes proactive strategies aren't enough, and school refusal has already set in. Maybe students start the year already avoiding school, or the refusal behavior develops despite your proactive efforts. In these cases, we need to shift to reactive strategies that focus on flexibility, empathy, and gradual reintegration.

Flexibility and Individualized Learning: One of the most critical elements of addressing school refusal is to adapt to the students' needs. Not all students fit into the same mold, and research shows that a flexible and individualized approach to learning can be the most beneficial for students with school refusal (Bernstein & Garfinkel, 2017). Here are a few ways to make school more manageable for these students:

- **Personalized Learning Plans:** Create personalized learning plans that accommodate the students' specific needs. This could include using choice boards, incorporating the students' interests into assignments, or varying the amount and type of work they're given. For example, if students love animals, you could incorporate that interest into their reading assignments.

- **Varied Assessment Methods:** Offer alternatives to traditional testing, like project-based assessments or oral presentations. Reducing the pressure of high-stakes testing can make school feel less intimidating for students with anxiety.

- **Flexibility in Attendance:** Consider flexible attendance options, like blended learning or remote participation. For students who are actively refusing school, this can be a short-term solution that helps ease them back into the classroom environment. Maybe they start by completing some assignments from home and gradually increase their time spent at school. These assignments can be work that the class has been completing in school, similar assignments to ones that they had been working on when they were in the classroom, or online platforms that provide instruction. Some examples include Khan Academy, BrainPOP, and reading work from the University of Florida Literacy Institute. While supporting students is incredibly important, the goal is not to additionally exhaust yourself as the teacher to implement these flexible strategies.

- **Gradual Reintegration: Taking Small Steps Toward Success:** When a student has been out of school for a while, jumping straight back into full-day attendance is usually overwhelming. Instead, a gradual reintegration plan can be far more successful. A phased approach can be essential and help to avoid overwhelming the child. Here's how you might structure it:

  - **Start Small:** Begin with short, positive experiences at school. This could be a visit to the classroom for a fun activity without the expectation of staying the whole day. The goal is to help the student rebuild positive associations with school.

  - **Incremental Increases:** Slowly extend the student's time at school as their comfort level grows. You might start with a half-day and gradually increase to full-day attendance. Having a data collection system to track their progress can help the team determine when to make these changes.

- **Providing Incentives:** While I'm not always a fan of physical incentives, sometimes a tangible reward can be a motivating factor for students with severe school refusal. This could be something like earning a special spot in the classroom, choosing a class activity, or a small reward to take home.

The Power of Proactive and Reactive Strategies

When classrooms utilize these proactive strategies, we can really curb school refusal before it spirals out of control. The beauty of the 2 × 10 strategy, collaboration with stakeholders, and mindfulness education is that these approaches not only reduce the possibility of school refusal developing but also help students build essential skills in emotional regulation, coping, and self-awareness.

However, when school refusal is already entrenched, reactive strategies like gradual reintegration and flexible attendance plans offer students a chance to rebuild their relationship with school in a safe, supportive way. By balancing empathy with structure, and support with accountability, we can guide students through their challenges with school refusal and set them up for long-term success. It's not easy, but with persistence and the right approach, we can make school a place where they feel comfortable and confident again.

Case Study #1

Raven is a 9-year-old fourth-grade student at Huron Elementary School. Recently, Raven's teacher, Ms. Hayes, raised concerns about Raven's inconsistent attendance and difficulty engaging in class. Raven is often late to school, and her father reports that this is because she does not want to come to school. When Raven does arrive late, it typically takes her between 45 minutes to an hour to warm up and start participating in class. Ms. Hayes is worried that this behavior could escalate into full-blown school refusal if not addressed quickly.

Raven's academic struggles, particularly in reading, have been an ongoing concern. She is currently in the process of being evaluated for a possible learning disability in reading. Additionally, Raven has on-again, off-again friendships with the girls in her class and has not fully "clicked" with Ms. Hayes, which is thought to contribute to her reluctance to attend school.

Initial Observations

Ms. Hayes noticed that Raven seemed hesitant and withdrawn during literacy activities, often looking around to see if other students were finishing before she even started. She also observed that Raven frequently needed to leave the classroom for reading support, which seemed to create tension with her peers. Some of the girls in the class had asked Ms. Hayes where Raven was going and seemed skeptical and confused about her whereabouts.

The inconsistency in Raven's attendance and engagement made it difficult for Ms. Hayes to fully assess her academic levels, particularly in reading. Raven's social relationships also seemed fragile, with conflicts arising and resolving quickly, leaving her without a stable group of friends. Ms. Hayes began to worry that Raven's reluctance to come to school and her difficulty connecting with her peers might lead to more significant behavioral issues, like school refusal.

Problem-Solving Approach

Recognizing the need for a comprehensive approach, Ms. Hayes collaborated with the school counselor, Mrs. Blake, and the school psychologist, Dr. Williams, to address Raven's academic and social challenges. Together, they developed a plan to support Raven's emotional well-being, build stronger relationships, and improve her engagement in school.

Team Collaboration

1. **Ms. Hayes (Teacher):** Focused on building a stronger relationship with Raven and implementing classroom strategies to support her academically and socially.
2. **Mrs. Blake (School Counselor):** Provided emotional support for Raven, addressing her reluctance to attend school and working on social skills development.
3. **Dr. Williams (School Psychologist):** Assisted with the evaluation process for a possible learning disability in reading and provided input on current interventions.

Designing the Intervention

The team developed an intervention plan to address Raven's academic, social, and emotional needs. The goal was to build her confidence, improve her social relationships, and create a more positive association with school.

Components of the Intervention

1. **Relationship-Building:**
   - **2 × 10 Strategy:** Ms. Hayes implemented the 2 × 10 relationship-building strategy, developed by Dr. Raymond Wlodkowski, to strengthen her connection with Raven. For 10 consecutive days, Ms. Hayes set aside two minutes each day to engage in a personal, non-academic conversation with Raven. The goal was to build rapport and show genuine interest in Raven as a person.
2. **Social and Emotional Support:**
   - **Counseling Sessions:** Mrs. Blake provided weekly 1:1 counseling sessions for six weeks to help Raven develop coping strategies for managing social anxiety and academic frustrations. These

sessions also focused on improving Raven's social skills and navigating conflicts with her peers. In the sessions Mrs. Blake explicitly discussed how school attendance plays a role, even tardies.

3. **Academic Support:**
   - **Reading Intervention:** Dr. Williams recommended a tailored reading intervention plan to address Raven's specific learning needs prior to this when they had reviewed the school reading data. Raven was engaging with daily one-on-one reading intervention support from Ms. Carlson, the reading interventionist, until her evaluation concluded to determine if she was eligible for an Individualized Education Program (IEP).
   - **Classroom Accommodations:** Ms. Hayes implemented classroom accommodations, such as allowing Raven to use audiobooks or providing additional time for reading tasks. These accommodations helped reduce Raven's anxiety around reading activities.

Implementing the Intervention

With the intervention plan in place, Ms. Hayes began implementing the new strategies in her classroom. The goal was to create a more supportive and positive environment for Raven, both academically and socially.

Personalized Support for Raven

Raven was initially hesitant to participate in the daily conversations with Ms. Hayes. She responded with brief answers and didn't seem interested in engaging. However, Ms. Hayes remained consistent, finding small ways to connect with Raven each day, whether through talking about Raven's favorite TV show, asking about her weekend, or discussing her hobbies. Given her initial reluctance to engage in these conversations, the intervention lasted longer than the standard 10 days. Ms. Hayes continued the daily conversations until Raven began to open up and feel more comfortable.

The turning point came when Raven confided in Ms. Hayes during one of their daily check-ins. She shared that she was embarrassed about how hard it was for her to read and that the girls in the class had been asking her why she had to leave for reading support. This admission helped Ms. Hayes better understand the depth of Raven's anxiety and reluctance to come to school. This also gave her more information on how she could educate her class.

Educating the Class

Ms. Hayes took steps to create a more inclusive and supportive classroom culture. She held class discussions about the importance of kindness, understanding, and respecting each other's differences. These discussions were framed around building a classroom community where everyone felt valued and supported. She used books and hypothetical social problem-solving scenarios to have students consider what they would do in situations where a student needed accommodations, modifications, or paraprofessional support. This helped the class build empathy and an understanding for the different paths students take in school.

Monitoring Progress

The team closely monitored Raven's progress through regular check-ins and data collection. They tracked her attendance, participation in class, and social interactions with peers.

Initial Challenges

Raven's progress was slow at first. Despite the comprehensive plan, she continued to arrive late to school frequently, and it still took her a considerable amount of time to warm up to participating in class. She was also cautious about opening up in counseling sessions and often appeared to downplay her feelings.

Positive Developments

Eventually, the combination of consistent relationship-building and tailored academic support began to make a difference. Raven eventually did become eligible for an IEP under the learning disability category and was given a comprehensive set of reading goals. With her IEP, Raven became connected to her case manager and special education teacher, Mrs. Bowman, whom she connected with immediately. Raven started arriving at school on time more regularly and became more engaged in class activities. The times that Raven did arrive tardy, it took her much less time than prior to warm up. The daily conversations with Ms. Hayes helped her feel more connected to her teacher, and she began to view school as a more supportive and less intimidating environment.

Raven also started to use the coping strategies she had learned in counseling sessions. For example, when she felt overwhelmed by a reading task, she would use deep breathing exercises to calm herself before asking Ms. Hayes for help. This shift in behavior marked significant progress in Raven's ability to manage her anxiety. Mrs. Bowman was also able to reinforce these strategies in their sessions, which helped with reinforcing and solidifying the skills.

Adjustments and Future Steps

Based on the evaluation, the team identified areas for further improvement and considered expanding some of the strategies to benefit other students in the class.

Continuous Support for Raven

- **Ongoing Reading Support:** Raven continued to receive tailored reading interventions that were now more robust and tailored after qualifying for an IEP.

- **Social Skills Development:** Mrs. Bowman began to encourage Raven to advocate for her needs, even in social situations. As her case manager, she continued to monitor her ability to navigate tricky situations to determine if she might benefit from an evaluation to add social work services to her IEP.

Conclusion

Raven's story highlights the importance of understanding the underlying causes of a student's reluctance to attend school and the power of building strong relationships to address those challenges. By implementing the 2 × 10 strategy, persevering with academic support, and fostering a more inclusive classroom environment, the school team was able to help Raven feel more confident, supported, and engaged in her learning. While the journey required patience and persistence, the positive outcomes really show the effectiveness of a collaborative, research-backed approach to addressing student behavior before it gets a chance to spiral.

Case Study #2

Jacob is a 10-year-old fifth-grade student who was diagnosed with an emotional behavioral disorder (EBD). This year, he is new to Oakwood Elementary School, having transferred after a history of significant school refusal behaviors at his previous school. Jacob has a long history of avoiding school due to anxiety, and his struggles with emotional regulation have led to difficulties in both academic and social settings. His IEP outlines the supports for his emotional and behavioral needs, but these supports had been inconsistently implemented in the past because of his frequent absences.

On the first day of school, Jacob arrived on time, but on the second day, he was two hours late and reluctant to enter the building.

The school principal, Mr. Harrison, had to escort him to his classroom, and Jacob remained visibly anxious throughout the day. Unfortunately, Jacob refused to come to school for the remainder of the week, reigniting concerns about his school refusal behavior.

Problem-Solving Approach

Recognizing the need for a comprehensive and carefully designed plan, Jacob's case manager, Ms. Thompson, and his classroom teacher, Mr. Brown, convened a meeting with the school social worker, Mrs. Stevens, the school psychologist, Dr. Ramirez, and the school principal, Mr. Harrison. Together, they began brainstorming strategies to support Jacob's emotional and behavioral needs while addressing his school refusal. They also sought input from Jacob's parents, who provided valuable insights into his history and triggers.

Team Collaboration

1. **Ms. Thompson (Special Education Teacher and Case Manager):** Focused on supporting Jacob's emotional and behavioral needs, as outlined in his IEP, and implementing personalized interventions.

2. **Mr. Brown (General Education Teacher):** Worked on creating a welcoming classroom environment and ensuring that Jacob had access to academic materials when he was able to attend.

3. **Mrs. Stevens (School Social Worker):** Provided emotional support and worked with Jacob on anxiety-reduction strategies.

4. **Dr. Ramirez (School Psychologist):** Assisted with the evaluation process and guided the team in developing interventions to address Jacob's anxiety and school refusal.

5. **Mr. Harrison (Principal):** Coordinated communication with Jacob's family and helped implement logistical aspects of Jacob's gradual reentry plan.

Designing the Intervention

The team developed a comprehensive intervention plan that focused on gradually reintroducing Jacob to the school environment in a way that minimized his anxiety and built positive associations with attending school.

Components of the Intervention

1. **Gradual Reentry Plan:**
   - **Short Daily Attendance:** The team decided to start with short, positive experiences at school to help Jacob build comfort with the environment. Initially, Jacob would attend school for just 30 minutes each day. The goal was to create positive associations with school without overwhelming him. They would determine criteria that would guide the attendance length and when and how his day would become longer.
   - **Positive Reinforcement:** Each successful day at school, no matter how short, was celebrated. Jacob earned small rewards for attending, and his progress was tracked to help him see his improvements over time.

2. **Increased Support through IEP Revisions:**
   - **Shared Paraprofessional:** The team reconvened and reopened Jacob's IEP to increase his supports. They added a shared paraprofessional to work closely with Jacob during the school day, providing additional adult support and helping him navigate transitions.
   - **Flexibility in Programming:** Jacob's schedule was adjusted to provide more breaks and quiet time. The team worked to create a flexible schedule that allowed Jacob to build his stamina for attending school without feeling overwhelmed.

3. **2 × 10 Relationship-Building Strategy:**
   - **Daily Conversations:** The paraprofessional assigned to Jacob began implementing the 2 × 10 strategy with him each day upon his arrival. These two-minute conversations took place in the school foyer before Jacob even entered the classroom. The goal was to create a positive, low-pressure interaction with a trusted adult, helping Jacob feel more comfortable before transitioning into the classroom.

4. **Social and Emotional Support:**
   - **Individual Social Work Sessions:** Mrs. Stevens provided weekly sessions to work with Jacob on managing his anxiety and emotional regulation. She taught Jacob coping strategies, such as deep breathing and grounding exercises, to help him manage his emotions.
   - **School-Based Therapy:** Dr. Ramirez also provided support by conducting school-based therapy sessions that focused on building Jacob's resilience and reducing his anxiety around school.

Implementing the Intervention

With the intervention plan in place, the team began implementing the gradual reentry process for Jacob. The focus was on creating a supportive environment that would allow Jacob to gradually increase his time at school without triggering his anxiety.

Gradual Reentry and Early Challenges

Initially, Jacob struggled with the gradual reentry process. For the first three weeks, he attended school for only 30 minutes each day. During this time, he remained resistant to staying longer and frequently expressed a desire to leave as soon as his short time was up. Despite the team's best efforts, Jacob's progress was slow, and the team had to remain patient and consistent in its approach.

The paraprofessional's implementation of the 2 × 10 strategy also took time to yield any noticeable results. Jacob was initially unresponsive to the daily conversations, offering silence or short answers and showing little interest in engaging. However, the paraprofessional remained persistent, finding small ways to connect with Jacob through discussions about his interests, such as his favorite video games and animals.

Monitoring Progress

The team closely monitored Jacob's progress through regular check-ins and data collection. They tracked his attendance, participation in class, and emotional regulation throughout the day. Communication with Jacob's parents was ongoing, and they provided feedback on Jacob's behavior and emotional state at home.

Initial Challenges

For the first few weeks, Jacob's attendance remained limited to 30-minute increments, and he showed little interest in extending his time at school. The team recognized that this was part of the process and continued to implement the gradual reentry plan with patience and consistency. They emphasized the importance of positive reinforcement and made sure that Jacob felt supported during his short time at school.

Positive Developments

After three weeks, small but noticeable changes began to emerge. Jacob started to engage more during his daily conversations with the paraprofessional. The consistent 2 × 10 relationship-building strategy began to pay off, as Jacob opened up about his feelings of anxiety and began to express a growing sense of comfort with the school environment.

As Jacob's anxiety gradually decreased, he started participating in classroom activities during his short time at school. He began to complete small academic tasks, such as answering a question or working on a brief assignment. He began to talk about his love of math, which no one had identified prior. Encouraged by these positive changes, the team decided to increase his time at school to one hour per day.

The transition to attending school for an hour each day was successful. Jacob's anxiety continued to decrease, and he began participating more consistently in classroom activities. With the paraprofessional's support, Jacob was able to navigate transitions more smoothly, and his emotional regulation improved. The gradual increase in his time at school allowed Jacob to build confidence and develop positive associations with the school environment, especially his 5th grade classroom.

Over the course of six months, Jacob began attending school for 100% of the day. It was noted that this was the first time in three years that Jacob had spent an entire day at school.

Adjustments and Future Steps

Based on information from data collection, the team identified areas for continued support and considered expanding some of the strategies to benefit other students in the school.

Continuous Support for Jacob

- **Ongoing Paraprofessional Support:** Jacob continued to receive support from the paraprofessional to help him navigate the school day and manage his emotional regulation. The team planned to gradually reduce the paraprofessional's involvement as Jacob became more independent.
- **Continued Counseling:** Mrs. Stevens and Dr. Ramirez continued to provide regular sessions to support Jacob's emotional well-being and help him build resilience.

Conclusion

Jacob's story highlights the importance of a collaborative and gradual approach to addressing school refusal and EBDs. It really shows the importance of patience and sticking with your plan. By implementing a carefully structured reentry plan, increasing supports through his IEP, and fostering strong relationships through the 2 × 10 strategy, the school team was able to help Jacob build positive associations with school and improve his attendance and engagement. While the journey required tremendous patience and flexibility, the positive outcomes demonstrated the effectiveness of a supportive, research-backed approach to meeting the needs of students with complex emotional and behavioral challenges.

CHAPTER FOUR

Helplessness

HELPLESSNESS IN students can be one of the most challenging behaviors for teachers to address. Is it because it feels so frustrating as a teacher to witness? Or because it can be so hard to reverse? Maybe both. When students display helplessness, they are often disengaged from learning and seem to have given up before they've even tried. This behavior can manifest as an unwillingness to attempt tasks, frequently asking for help before even starting or expressing a belief that they "just can't do it."

Witnessing this can be disheartening for teachers. You're standing there, offering support, guidance, and encouragement, yet students continue to reject it, locked in a mindset that they are destined to fail no matter what they do. It's more than just a passing feeling of frustration. It's a deep-seated belief in their own inability, and recognizing this as a barrier to learning is crucial. Helplessness undermines students' sense of agency and confidence, making it difficult for them to engage with the content and make even the smallest academic gains.

Helplessness and Emotional Regulation

It's important to know that helplessness is often linked to a lack of emotional regulation. When students feel overwhelmed by a task or situation, they may respond by withdrawing, thinking no matter what they do, they will fail. This sense of helplessness can become a self-fulfilling prophecy, where students no longer believe in their own ability to succeed, which in turn negatively impacts their learning and engagement.

Why is this happening? Let's break it down. Think of the brain as a circuit board. When faced with challenges that seem insurmountable, the brain's stress response kicks in—what we commonly refer to as "fight, flight, or freeze." For students displaying helplessness, their brains often enter the "freeze" mode. This response can look like giving up, refusing to try, or asking for help before even attempting anything. It's a protective mechanism to avoid failure or discomfort.

But here's the kicker: These students are not choosing helplessness. Dr. Lori Desautels, an expert in educational neuroscience, emphasizes that the brain's stress response plays a significant role in students' feelings of helplessness. Their brains are wired to protect them from the emotional discomfort of perceived failure. This is why telling them to "just try harder" or "you can do it" rarely works. They are stuck in a mindset where they truly believe they cannot succeed.

Causes and Triggers of Helplessness in Students

Understanding the root of helplessness is essential for addressing this behavior effectively. Kristin Souers and Pete Hall, authors of *Fostering Resilient Learners*, explain that students who exhibit helplessness often do so because of past experiences that have eaten away at their confidence and sense of control. These experiences can range from trauma, inconsistent support systems, or repeated failures that have led to a belief that their efforts don't matter.

Imagine students who have consistently struggled with reading. Year after year, despite trying their best, they continue to fall behind.

At some point, it becomes easier to stop trying. Why attempt something when you're convinced it will only end in failure?

Trauma, in particular, plays a major role in shaping a student's response to challenge. Dr. Bruce Perry, a renowned expert on childhood trauma, explains that students who have experienced trauma or instability in their lives are particularly prone to feelings of helplessness. The unpredictability of their environment can lead to a sense of learned helplessness, where they believe their actions have little effect on the outcomes they experience. This belief often carries over into the classroom, making it extra challenging for them to engage in tasks that require effort and persistence.

One example might be students who have lived in multiple foster homes. Their environment has been chaotic and unstable, and as a result, they've developed a belief that they have little control over their life. This belief spills into the classroom, where students become disengaged, asking for help before even trying or refusing to start a task at all. They're not just being stubborn—they're grappling with a deep-seated belief that their actions won't make a difference.

Proactive Strategies for Addressing Helplessness

So, what can we do to help these students? Addressing helplessness in the classroom requires a compassionate and strategic approach. We need to provide students with opportunities to rebuild their confidence and sense of agency. But how? Let's dive into some research-backed strategies to proactively support students who exhibit helplessness.

Crafting Multi-Step Plans: Breaking Tasks Into Bite-Sized Pieces

One of the most effective ways to combat helplessness is by helping students experience success through achievable goals. Kristin Souers and Pete Hall emphasize the importance of creating small, manageable steps for students to build their confidence. By breaking down tasks into smaller, more attainable goals, students can experience success incrementally, which can help rebuild their belief in their abilities.

Here's a practical example: let's say students are struggling with a complex math problem. Rather than focusing on the entire problem, the teacher can help the students tackle it one step at a time. The first step might be identifying what the problem is asking, the second could be setting up the equation, and so on. Celebrating each small success along the way can provide the students with the encouragement they need to keep going.

This strategy is crucial because it doesn't just help the students complete the task—it helps them regulate their emotions. Dr. Desautels highlights that when students achieve success, even in small steps, it reduces the brain's stress response. The students' nervous system calms, and they feel more capable of tackling the next step. It's all about creating a positive feedback loop: Success breeds confidence, which in turn makes students more willing to engage in future tasks.

Explicit Teaching of Problem-Solving and Resilience Skills

Another critical strategy for addressing helplessness is teaching students how to solve problems and build resilience. We often assume that students know how to break down problems or persevere when things get tough, but many students need explicit instruction in these skills.

For instance, a teacher might use a structured approach like "think-alouds" to model problem-solving strategies in real-time. As the teacher works through a difficult task, the students verbalize their thought process: "Hmm, this problem looks tough, but let me break it down. First, I'll see what information I already know, and then I'll figure out what I still need to do." This simple strategy shows students that challenges are a normal part of learning and that there are ways to approach difficult tasks.

Dr. Carol Dweck's work on growth mindset also ties in here. When we teach students that effort and persistence are key components of success, they start to shift their mindset from "I can't do this" to "I can't do this yet, but I'm learning." By incorporating growth mindset language into everyday classroom interactions, we're reinforcing the idea that abilities can be developed with effort, which directly counters the fixed mindset that fuels helplessness.

Try out these growth mindset conversation cards to help build this skill set within your students by using the QR code below.

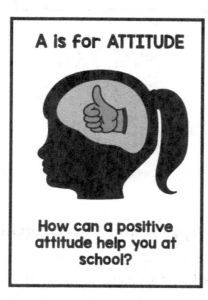

(Continued)

Emotional Support and Encouragement

This may seem obvious, but emotional support is a powerful antidote to helplessness. Dr. Bruce Perry suggests that creating a predictable and stable environment can help students regain a sense of control. When students know what to expect, they feel less anxious and more willing to engage in learning tasks. Predictability reduces anxiety, and when students feel safe and supported, they are more likely to try.

Take classroom routines, for example. Having a predictable structure for how lessons begin, progress, and end can reduce anxiety in students who feel overwhelmed by change or uncertainty. If students know that math class always starts with five minutes of quiet reflection followed by a group activity, they are less likely to feel anxious and more likely to engage. Predictability provides a sense of security, which is key for students prone to helplessness.

Additionally, providing students with opportunities to talk about their feelings, validating their emotions, and offering reassurance can help them feel more confident in their ability to tackle challenges. Simple gestures like checking in with students during independent work, offering words of encouragement or just acknowledging their frustration can go a long way. For students stuck in helplessness, hearing "I see you're having a hard time, and that's okay. Let's figure this out together" can make all the difference.

Creating an Environment that Fosters Problem-Solving

To support students dealing with helplessness, it's essential to create a classroom environment that fosters problem-solving and perseverance. This doesn't mean that every task needs to be a breeze, but it does mean that students need to feel safe taking risks and making mistakes. Here are a few practical ways to create that environment:

- **Normalize Struggle:** Students need to understand that struggle is part of learning. Display posters with growth mindset phrases like "Mistakes are proof that you're trying," or "Effort is more important than ability." Use these phrases regularly in your teaching, especially when students face challenges.
- **Celebrate Effort:** Acknowledge and celebrate students' efforts, even when they don't achieve immediate success. For example, instead of

just praising a student for getting the right answer, praise their persistence: "I love how you stuck with that problem, even when it was tricky. That's real learning."

- **Provide Time for Reflection:** Encourage students to reflect on their learning process. After completing a challenging task, ask them to think about what strategies worked, what didn't, and how they overcame obstacles. This reflection helps students recognize their own problem-solving abilities, which in turn builds resilience.

Monitoring Progress and Adjusting Strategies

Addressing helplessness is not a one-and-done solution. It's an ongoing process that requires regular monitoring and adjustments. Teachers should keep track of how students are responding to the strategies in place. Are they starting to show more willingness to try? Are they asking for help less frequently? If progress is slow, that's okay. What's important is that students are moving in the right direction.

If you notice that a particular strategy isn't working, don't be afraid to adjust. Maybe breaking tasks into smaller steps needs more scaffolding, or perhaps the students need additional emotional support before they're ready to tackle academic challenges. Flexibility and responsiveness are key when working with students who struggle with helplessness.

Conclusion: Empowering Students Through Small Wins and Big Support

Addressing helplessness in the classroom is complex, but it's absolutely essential. Students who feel helpless are not just avoiding tasks—they're struggling with deep-rooted beliefs about their own abilities.

By recognizing the emotional and neurological triggers behind this behavior, we can provide students with the tools they need to rebuild their confidence and regain a sense of agency.

From crafting multi-step plans to teaching explicit problem-solving skills and providing emotional support, we have the power to help students overcome feelings of helplessness. With patience, persistence, and the right strategies in place, we can help them believe in their ability to succeed—and there's nothing more rewarding than watching a student move from "I can't" to "I can."

Case Study #1

Lila is a 7-year-old second-grade student at Willow Grove Elementary School. Lila's teacher, Ms. Harper, has worked hard to develop a classroom culture centered around growth mindset and resilience, encouraging students to embrace challenges and persist through difficulties. However, Lila consistently exhibits behaviors that suggest a deep-seated sense of helplessness and often an almost immediate fixed mindset. Before she even begins a task, Lila often raises her hand, stating that she needs help or that she cannot do it. This pattern of behavior has become a significant barrier to her learning and engagement in the classroom.

Ms. Harper observed that Lila frequently gives up at the first sign of difficulty, often refusing to attempt tasks independently. This behavior is particularly evident during math and writing activities, where Lila seems to lack confidence in her abilities. Despite repeated encouragement and reassurance, Lila's immediate reaction to new or challenging tasks is to seek help or avoid the task altogether. Ms. Harper is concerned that Lila's helplessness is preventing her from developing the problem-solving skills and resilience that are crucial for academic success.

Problem-Solving Approach

Recognizing that Lila's behavior was not improving with general classroom strategies, Ms. Harper decided to seek additional support. She scheduled a meeting with the school's Student Support Team (SST), which includes the school counselor, Ms. Lee, the school psychologist, Dr. Patel, and the special education teacher, Mr. Miller. The goal of the meeting was to discuss Lila's behavior, identify possible underlying causes, and develop a targeted intervention plan to address her needs.

Ms. Harper also reached out to Lila's parents, Mr. and Mrs. Evans, to discuss their observations at home and gain their input on the potential causes of Lila's helplessness. Lila's parents expressed concern about her lack of confidence and shared that she often exhibits similar behaviors at home, particularly when faced with new or challenging tasks. They were eager to collaborate with the school to support Lila's development of independence and problem-solving skills.

Team Collaboration

1. **Ms. Harper (General Education Teacher):** Provided insights into Lila's behavior in the classroom and her attempts to foster a growth mindset.
2. **Ms. Lee (School Counselor):** Offered strategies for addressing Lila's emotional needs and promoting self-confidence.
3. **Dr. Patel (School Psychologist):** Assisted in understanding potential psychological factors contributing to Lila's helplessness and recommended evidence-based interventions.
4. **Mr. Miller (Special Education Teacher):** Provided expertise in differentiated instruction and scaffolding techniques to support Lila's academic growth.
5. **Mr. and Mrs. Evans (Parents):** Shared their observations of Lila's behavior at home and collaborated on developing strategies to reinforce the intervention at home.

Designing the Intervention

After discussing Lila's behavior and reviewing relevant research, the team agreed that Lila's helplessness likely stemmed from a lack of confidence in her abilities and an over-reliance on adult support. This may have stemmed from adults jumping in to support her at earlier grades, and Lila becoming attached to that sense of assurance and attention from trusted adults. The team's primary goal was to help Lila develop independence and problem-solving skills by gradually increasing her ability to tackle tasks on her own.

The intervention plan included the following key components:

1. **Breaking Down Tasks:** Lila often felt overwhelmed by complex tasks, leading to her immediate requests for help. The team decided to break down challenging tasks into smaller, more manageable steps. This approach would help Lila focus on one step at a time, making the overall task feel less daunting. The use of graphic organizers would be a helpful tool for this as well.

2. **Explicit Teaching of Problem-Solving Skills:** Lila needed to learn specific strategies for approaching tasks independently. The team planned to teach Lila problem-solving skills explicitly, such as how to analyze a problem, identify possible solutions, and choose the best course of action.

3. **Positive Reinforcement:** The team agreed to use positive reinforcement to encourage Lila's independent efforts. Praise and small rewards like stamps and stickers would be given for attempts at independent work, even if she didn't get everything right on the first try.

4. **Parental Involvement:** Lila's parents would play a crucial role in reinforcing these strategies at home. They agreed to use similar approaches to encourage independence in tasks outside of school, such as homework and daily chores.

Implementing the Intervention

With the intervention plan in place, Ms. Harper began implementing the strategies in her classroom. She started by introducing the concept of breaking down tasks using a graphic organizer during whole-class instruction, using examples relevant to the day's lessons. Ms. Harper modeled how to approach a challenging task step by step, emphasizing the importance of persistence and celebrating small successes along the way.

Personalized Support

In addition to the classwide instruction, Ms. Harper provided Lila with personalized support. For instance, during math lessons, Ms. Harper would work with Lila to break down word problems into smaller steps. She used visual aids, such as checklists and graphic organizers, to help Lila organize her thoughts and approach the problems systematically.

Ms. Lee, the school counselor, also began meeting with Lila weekly to work on building her confidence and resilience. During these sessions, they practiced problem-solving strategies and discussed ways Lila could manage her feelings of frustration when faced with difficult tasks. Ms. Lee used role-playing scenarios to help Lila rehearse how to ask herself questions and seek out possible solutions before asking for help.

Educating the Class

Ms. Harper continued to reinforce the importance of a growth mindset in the classroom. She introduced the concept of "yet" to the students, encouraging them to think of challenges as opportunities to learn rather than as barriers. For example, instead of saying, "I can't do this," students were encouraged to say, "I can't do this yet." This language shift helped normalize the experience of struggling with a task and emphasized the importance of effort and persistence.

Ms. Harper also implemented a "Problem-Solvers" wall, where students could share examples of problems they had solved independently.

This visual reminder served as a source of inspiration and motivation for Lila and her classmates, reinforcing the idea that everyone can be a problem-solver with the right mindset and strategies.

Monitoring Progress

The team monitored Lila's progress through regular check-ins and data collection. Ms. Harper kept detailed notes on Lila's behavior during independent work times, noting instances where Lila attempted to solve problems on her own versus when she immediately asked for help. Ms. Lee continued to meet with Lila weekly, tracking her emotional growth and the development of her problem-solving skills.

Initial Challenges

Initially, Lila struggled to adapt to the new strategies. Despite the step-by-step guidance and explicit teaching of problem-solving skills, Lila continued to raise her hand frequently, asking for help before even attempting a task. She expressed frustration during her sessions with Ms. Lee, saying that she still didn't feel capable of completing the tasks on her own.

The team recognized that change would take time and that Lila needed consistent support and encouragement. They adjusted their approach by providing even more scaffolding during the early stages of the intervention, ensuring that Lila had the tools and confidence to take the first step independently.

Positive Developments

After several weeks of consistent implementation, Lila began to show signs of improvement. She started to use the problem-solving strategies taught by Ms. Lee more independently. For example, during a math lesson, Lila was observed quietly using her checklist to break down a word problem before raising her hand. When Ms. Harper approached her, Lila proudly showed that she had completed the first two steps on her own.

These small successes were celebrated both in the classroom and at home, reinforcing Lila's growing confidence. The positive reinforcement system proved effective, with Lila earning praise and small rewards for her independent efforts. Gradually, Lila's requests for help decreased, and she began to express more confidence in her abilities.

Adjustments and Future Steps

As Lila's confidence grew, the team made adjustments to the intervention plan to continue challenging her while providing the necessary support. They gradually reduced the level of scaffolding provided during tasks, encouraging Lila to take more initiative in problem-solving. The focus shifted from providing step-by-step guidance to encouraging Lila to independently identify when and how to use the strategies she had learned.

The team also introduced more complex tasks that required Lila to apply her problem-solving skills in new contexts. For example, in writing assignments, Lila was encouraged to use graphic organizers, a now familiar tool, to plan her stories independently. These tasks were designed to push Lila beyond her comfort zone while still providing the support she needed to succeed.

Continuous Support

The team recognized that Lila's progress was ongoing and that continuous support would be necessary to maintain her growth. Regular check-ins with Lila's parents ensured that the strategies used at school were reinforced at home. Ms. Harper and Ms. Lee continued to provide consistent encouragement and celebrate Lila's successes, no matter how small.

The school also considered incorporating similar problem-solving strategies into the curriculum for other students who might benefit from explicit instruction in resilience and independence. The success of the intervention with Lila highlighted the importance of addressing helplessness through a combination of targeted instruction, emotional support, and positive reinforcement.

Conclusion

Lila's story underscores the complexity of addressing helplessness in young students and the importance of a collaborative, research-based approach. Through the dedicated efforts of her teachers, school staff, and parents, Lila began to develop the confidence and problem-solving skills necessary to overcome her feelings of helplessness. By breaking down tasks, explicitly teaching problem-solving strategies, and providing continuous emotional support, the team was able to help Lila build the resilience she needed to succeed in the classroom

While Lila's journey required patience and persistence, the positive outcomes demonstrated the effectiveness of targeted interventions in addressing helplessness. This case study serves as a reminder that with the right support, students who struggle with helplessness can learn to embrace challenges, develop independence, and achieve academic success.

Case Study #2

David is an 11-year-old sixth-grade student at Green Valley. David's school has a push for all teachers to focus on classroom cultures of growth mindset and resilience, encouraging students to approach challenges with perseverance. Despite these efforts, David exhibits patterns of helplessness that significantly affect his learning and participation in class.

David often gives up before even starting tasks, expressing doubt about his abilities or stating that he "already knows how to do this." He alternates between two distinct behaviors: sometimes, he becomes very silly and distracts his classmates, while at other times, he becomes passive, putting his head down on his desk and disengaging completely.

These behaviors have created a barrier to his academic success and social success, and they disrupt the learning environment for his classmates.

Ms. Clark is David's homeroom teacher, and is concerned that David's helplessness is preventing him from developing the problem-solving skills and resilience that are essential for his academic and personal growth. Additionally, his fluctuating behaviors—ranging from silliness to disengagement—indicate that there may be underlying emotional or social factors contributing to his sense of helplessness.

Problem-Solving Approach

Recognizing that David's behavior could not be addressed solely through general classroom management strategies, Ms. Clark decided to involve other school staff and David's parents in the problem-solving process. She scheduled a meeting with the school's SST, which includes the school counselor, Ms. Lewis, the special education teacher, Mr. Jones, and the school psychologist, Dr. White. Ms. Clark also reached out to David's parents to gather more information about his behavior at home and their perspectives on his challenges in school.

David's parents shared that they had heard about David's silliness from past teachers, but that the other behaviors felt new to them. They did express concern about his fluctuating moods, noting that he could be cheerful and playful one moment but withdrawn and quiet the next.

Together, the team aimed to identify the root causes of David's helplessness and to develop an intervention that would empower him to approach tasks with more confidence and persistence.

Team Collaboration

The SST meeting included the following team members:

1. **Ms. Clark (General Education Teacher):** Provided insights into David's academic performance and classroom behavior, including his patterns of helplessness, distractibility, and disengagement.

2. **Ms. Lewis (School Counselor):** Offered strategies for addressing David's emotional needs and building his confidence in the classroom.

3. **Mr. Jones (Special Education Teacher):** Provided expertise in differentiated instruction and offered suggestions for academic interventions that could support David's learning.

4. **Dr. White (School Psychologist):** Assisted in understanding potential psychological factors contributing to David's helplessness and emotional regulation challenges.

5. **David's Parents:** Shared observations of David's behavior at home and collaborated on developing strategies to reinforce the intervention at home.

Designing the Intervention

The team discussed several possible reasons for David's helplessness, including anxiety about failure, low self-esteem, and difficulty with emotional regulation. They concluded that David's frequent avoidance of tasks was likely rooted in a fear of failure and a lack of confidence in his abilities. His silly and distracting behavior appeared to be a way to deflect attention from his struggles, while his passivity reflected a sense of defeat.

The goal of the intervention was to help David develop the skills and confidence needed to not only approach tasks independently but also with perseverance. The intervention would focus on providing David with structured support, gradually increasing his workload, and offering him choices to give him more control over his learning.

Components of the Intervention

1. **Small Group Work:** The team decided that David would benefit from working in a small group setting, where he could receive more individualized attention and feel less pressure. This setting would also allow him to observe and model the behavior of peers who were

more confident in tackling tasks. This could be as simple as a small group of students working together in a quiet spot in the classroom or hallway.

2. **Scaling Back and Gradually Increasing Workload:** To reduce David's sense of being overwhelmed, the team agreed to scale back the amount of work he was given initially. He would be provided with shorter, simpler tasks that were within his ability level, allowing him to experience success. As he gained confidence, the workload would gradually increase.

3. **Choice Boards:** The use of choice boards would give David more autonomy over his learning. Choice boards provide students with a variety of task options, allowing them to select activities that interest them or that they feel more comfortable completing. This strategy would help reduce David's anxiety by giving him a sense of control over the work he was assigned.

4. **Emotional Support:** Ms. Lewis would meet with David's homeroom class weekly to provide quick emotional regulation and self-confidence mini-lessons. These short lessons would focus on teaching all students strategies for managing frustration and building resilience, which would benefit all, while also providing David more targeted instruction.

5. **Parental Involvement:** David's parents would reinforce the interventions at home as applicable by using similar strategies, such as breaking down homework into smaller steps and providing choices for completing tasks. They would also use positive reinforcement to celebrate David's independent efforts at home.

Implementing the Intervention

Ms. Clark began implementing the intervention in her classroom. She assigned David to a small group where he could receive more individualized support as needed and have some appropriate peer models. She also introduced the concept of choice boards, allowing David to select from a variety of tasks each day. The tasks on the choice board ranged in difficulty, giving David the option to start with simpler activities and gradually work his way up to more challenging ones.

Personalized Support

Ms. Clark provided David with personalized support during small group work, helping him break down tasks into manageable steps. For example, during math lessons, she would guide David through the first few problems, then encourage him to attempt the next ones independently. As David demonstrated success with smaller tasks, Ms. Clark gradually increased the complexity of the work.

Ms. Lewis worked with David's class during weekly mini-lessons to help students practice identifying and managing feelings of frustration. They practiced deep breathing exercises and positive self-talk strategies that students could use when they felt overwhelmed by a task. Ms. Lewis also independently encouraged David to focus on the effort he put into tasks, rather than the outcome, reinforcing the idea that making mistakes is a natural part of learning.

Educating the Class

Ms. Clark continued to emphasize the importance of a growth mindset in the classroom. She used class discussions and activities to teach students about resilience, effort, and the value of learning from mistakes. This helped create a supportive environment where David—and his classmates—felt safe taking risks and trying new things.

Ms. Clark also introduced a "Success Wall" in the classroom, where students could post examples of challenges they had overcome. David was encouraged to contribute to the wall by sharing moments when he successfully completed a task he had initially found difficult.

Monitoring Progress

The team regularly monitored David's progress by tracking his engagement in class, his completion of independent tasks, and his behavior during small group work. Ms. Clark kept detailed notes on David's participation, noting whether he was attempting tasks on his own or continuing to seek help before starting. Ms. Lewis also helped Ms. Clark track David's emotional growth and his ability to manage frustration.

Initial Challenges

At first, David struggled to adapt to the new strategies. Despite the smaller tasks and choice boards, he continued to display helplessness by avoiding work and putting his head down. He was hesitant to engage with his small group and frequently claimed that he still didn't know how to complete the tasks even after receiving instruction. His silly behavior also persisted as he attempted to distract his peers and avoid confronting the work in front of him.

The team recognized that progress would take time and that David needed consistent encouragement and reinforcement. They remained patient and continued to implement the strategies, providing him with positive feedback for even the smallest attempts at independent work.

Positive Developments

After several weeks, small but significant changes began to emerge. David started to engage more with his choice boards, selecting tasks that he felt comfortable completing. He also began participating more in small group discussions and asking questions when he was unsure, rather than avoiding the task altogether.

Ms. Clark noticed that David's silly behavior had decreased, and he was spending more time focused on his work. During one math lesson, David successfully completed a set of problems on his own and proudly showed them to Ms. Clark. This moment marked a turning point in David's confidence as he began to realize that he was capable of completing tasks independently.

Adjustments and Future Steps

As David's confidence grew, the team made adjustments to the intervention plan to continue challenging him while providing the necessary support. They gradually increased the complexity of the tasks on his choice boards and reduced the amount of scaffolding provided during small group work. The goal was to help David develop more independence while maintaining the progress he had made.

Ms. Lewis continued to work with David on his emotional regulation and resilience by utilizing a check-in, check-out type system. Ms. Lewis and David saw one another each morning and at the end of the day. They began focused on more advanced strategies, such as setting personal goals and reflecting on his progress. These check-ins helped David build a sense of ownership over his learning and gave him the tools to persevere through challenges.

Continuous Support

The team recognized that David's progress was ongoing and that continuous support would be necessary to maintain his growth. Regular check-ins with David's parents ensured that the strategies used at school were reinforced at home. The school team also planned to provide David with additional support as he transitioned to seventh grade, ensuring that he would continue to build on the skills he had developed.

Conclusion

David's story highlights the complexity of addressing helplessness in students and the importance of a collaborative, multi-faceted approach. Through the dedicated efforts of his teachers, school staff, and parents, David began to develop the confidence and resilience needed to approach tasks independently. By breaking down tasks, providing choices, and offering continuous emotional support, the team was able to help David overcome his feelings of helplessness and re-engage in his learning.

While David's journey required patience and persistence, the positive outcomes demonstrated the effectiveness of targeted interventions in addressing helplessness. This story serves as a reminder that helplessness and other related behaviors are different for each child, and that they can become more nuanced and complicated with age. Regardless of the barriers, with the right support, students who struggle with helplessness can learn to embrace challenges, develop independence, and achieve academic success.

CHAPTER FIVE

Disruptive Behavior

CLASSROOMS CAN be vibrant, active spaces where students learn, interact, and grow. But when disruptive behavior occurs, it can derail that learning process for both the individual exhibiting the behavior and the rest of the class. Let's face it, managing disruptive behavior is challenging. It's exhausting, it's frustrating, and it sometimes feels like there's no end in sight. But with some shifts in how we approach it, along with strategies that take into account both the student and the whole classroom, we can navigate disruptions in a way that not only minimizes them but also creates better outcomes for all involved.

Recognizing Disruptive Behavior as a Barrier to Learning and Engagement

Disruptive behaviors act as barriers to learning because they interfere with both the flow of instruction and students' ability to focus. When students are outwardly disruptive—whether through talking out of turn, making loud noises, or engaging in off-task behavior—they pull the focus away from academic engagement. But here's the thing: Disruptive behaviors are often signals of unmet needs or dysregulated emotions rather than just simple misbehavior.

Dr. Lori Desautels, an expert in educational neuroscience, has taught us a lot about how disruptive behaviors can often be linked to dysregulated nervous systems. When students are unable to self-regulate, they may act out in ways that interrupt the flow of the classroom. This behavior is more than just an annoyance—it's a form of communication, signaling that the student's emotional or physiological needs are not being met. When we view disruptive behavior in this light, we begin to approach it differently, not as something to punish or eliminate but as something to understand and address.

Defining Disruptive Behaviors and Their Manifestations

Disruptive behaviors can look different in every classroom and for every student. It's not always the stereotypical "class clown" or the kid who's constantly making noise. Sometimes, it's subtler. Here are a few examples of what disruptive behavior might look like:

Talking out of turn: Interrupting the teacher or classmates by talking without permission.

Making noises: Engaging in loud or distracting sounds, such as tapping pencils, whistling, or banging on desks.

Off-task behavior: Not following the lesson or instructions, engaging in unrelated activities like doodling, playing with objects, or using technology inappropriately.

Defiance: Refusing to follow instructions or comply with classroom rules.

Physical disruptions: Moving around the room, pushing, or knocking over items.

Now, these behaviors aren't always done with the intention of disrupting the class. According to Dr. Mona Delahooke, who focuses on trauma-informed teaching, students often engage in disruptive behaviors because they're struggling with emotional dysregulation, sensory overload, or past trauma. These kids aren't just trying to be difficult—they're responding to internal states of stress or confusion, and their behavior is the only way they know how to communicate that.

Consequences of Disruption on Learning and Teaching

Let's talk about the ripple effect of disruptive behavior. It doesn't just impact the students who are exhibiting it—it affects the entire class. For the students, frequent disruptions create a cycle of negative interactions. Think about it: The more they disrupt, the more they are reprimanded, and the more they are reprimanded, the less they feel capable of engaging in the learning process. It becomes a vicious cycle, where learning takes a backseat to conflict.

For the rest of the class, disruptions can cause frustration, confusion, and disengagement. Dr. Bruce Perry, a leading expert on childhood trauma and brain development, emphasizes that disruptions in the classroom can dysregulate the nervous systems of other students, making it harder for them to focus and learn. A single disruptive behavior can shift the emotional climate of the room, pulling everyone's attention away from the task at hand.

Teachers, too, bear the brunt of these behaviors. Constant interruptions can lead to teacher stress and burnout. It's tough to maintain the energy and patience required to manage a classroom when you're constantly putting out fires. And when teachers spend more time addressing disruptive behaviors, they have less time to focus on instruction and building positive relationships with students.

Techniques for Managing Disruptive Behavior

So, how do we address disruptive behavior in a way that's effective but also compassionate? The goal is to manage disruptions in a way that keeps the classroom running smoothly while supporting the individual student. Let's explore some strategies that work.

Implementing Consistent Behavior Management Strategies

Consistency is key when it comes to managing disruptive behavior. Students need clear expectations and predictable consequences for their actions. Dr. Lori Desautels emphasizes that consistent routines and expectations help regulate students' nervous systems by creating a sense of safety and predictability. When students know what's expected of them and what will happen if they don't follow through, they're less likely to act out.

One proactive approach is to establish classroom norms at the beginning of the year and review them regularly. These norms should focus on positive behaviors, like active listening and respectful communication, rather than simply outlining what students shouldn't do. Instead of having a list of "don'ts," why not create a list of "dos" that promote the behaviors you want to see?

For example, instead of "Don't talk while the teacher is talking," you might have "Respect others by listening when they are speaking." It's a small shift in language, but it focuses the conversation on what students *should* be doing.

Another great tool is the Classroom Charter, which comes from the RULER framework developed by Dr. Marc Brackett and the Yale Center for Emotional Intelligence. A Classroom Charter involves the students in deciding on five feelings words that describe how they want to feel in the classroom. It could be words like "safe," "heard," "respected," "engaged," and "calm." Then, the class collectively comes up with actions it can take to make sure everyone experiences those feelings. This process not only gives students ownership but also ties emotions to classroom behavior, which is a powerful way to manage disruptive behaviors.

Using Proximity and Non-Verbal Cues for Redirection

Disruptive behaviors can sometimes be managed without calling out the student or disrupting the flow of instruction. Using proximity and non-verbal cues is an effective way to redirect students without drawing attention to their behavior.

Dr. Mona Delahooke emphasizes the importance of non-verbal communication when supporting students with behavioral challenges. Let's say students start tapping their pencil loudly or are getting fidgety. Instead of stopping the lesson to address it, try moving closer to the student. Often, just being near them can help refocus their attention. Non-verbal cues like a gentle touch on their desk, making eye contact, or using a hand signal can be enough to stop the behavior before it escalates.

What's great about this strategy is that it doesn't embarrass the student or interrupt the lesson for everyone else. It's a subtle way to let the student know they're off track and bring them back without making them feel singled out.

Engaging Students in Meaningful Activities to Maintain Focus

One of the most effective ways to prevent disruptive behavior is by keeping students engaged in meaningful activities. When students are fully engaged, they're less likely to become distracted or disruptive. Dr. Marc Brackett suggests that teachers can help students stay focused by incorporating activities that are emotionally engaging and relevant to their interests.

Think about your classroom—are the students just passively listening to the lesson, or are they actively participating? Hands-on learning, group work, and giving students choices can make all the difference in engagement levels. For example, using choice boards or project-based learning allows students to have a say in what they're doing. When students feel a sense of autonomy over their work, they're more invested and less likely to disrupt.

For students who need a little extra support, personalize the content. Maybe they're obsessed with dinosaurs or superheroes. Find ways to weave their interests into the material. Something as simple as incorporating a favorite cartoon character into a math problem or letting them draw their answers can keep them on task.

Dr. Bruce Perry adds that creating an emotionally safe learning environment fosters engagement. When students feel like they belong and their contributions matter, they're more likely to exhibit positive behaviors. Teachers can build this sense of community through collaboration, peer support, and positive reinforcement. Simple shared experiences, like watching a funny video together or playing a class game, can create bonds that help students feel like they're part of something bigger. When students feel safe and supported, they're less likely to disrupt.

Common Challenges in Managing Class Disruptions

Managing disruptive behavior is a journey, not a destination. Even with all the best strategies, challenges will arise. Let's break down some of the common hurdles teachers face and how we can navigate them.

1. **Underlying Emotional and Psychological Needs:** Some students disrupt the classroom because of deeper emotional or psychological issues, like anxiety, trauma, or ADHD. Dr. Mona Delahooke highlights that these behaviors are forms of communication. Students might not know how to express what they need, so they act out. That's why it's crucial to address the root cause of the behavior, whether it's providing more sensory breaks, offering flexible seating, or creating tailored behavior plans.

2. **Teacher Stress and Burnout:** Managing disruptive behavior day in and day out can be draining. It's essential that teachers take care of themselves, too. Dr. Lori Desautels advises teachers to prioritize self-care and lean on colleagues for support. Whether it's talking to a school counselor or taking a few minutes to regroup during planning periods, teachers need to practice what we preach to our students: self-regulation and taking care of ourselves.

3. **Inconsistent Application of Strategies:** One of the most common challenges is inconsistency. If classroom expectations and consequences aren't applied consistently, students get mixed messages about what's acceptable. It's important to be predictable, not just in your classroom but across the whole school. This is where school-wide behavior plans can come in handy. When everyone's on the same page, students know exactly what to expect.

4. **Time and Patience:** Changing disruptive behavior is not an overnight fix. It's a process that requires time and patience. You might not see big changes immediately, but that doesn't mean the strategies aren't working. It's essential to celebrate small victories along the way and remember that progress, no matter how slow, is still progress.

Conclusion

Disruptive behavior in the classroom can be a significant barrier to learning, but with the right mindset and strategies, it's manageable. Recognizing disruptive behavior as a form of communication is the first step in addressing it. By implementing consistent behavior management strategies, using proximity and non-verbal cues, and keeping students engaged in meaningful activities, we can create a classroom environment that minimizes disruptions and supports all learners.

At the heart of it, disruptive behaviors don't need to be just obstacles to overcome—they can be authentic opportunities to connect with students on a deeper level. When we approach these behaviors with empathy and understanding, we not only manage the disruptions but also foster stronger relationships and create a more inclusive, supportive learning environment for everyone.

Case Study #1

Amelia is a 9-year-old third-grade student at Hilltop Elementary School. Amelia is very athletic, loves playing soccer, and reports that science is her favorite subject. Since third grade has begun, she has been exhibiting highly disruptive behavior in the classroom on a daily basis. Her teachers have reported a range of disruptive actions, including frequent blurting out, leaving her seat during instruction, making loud noises, and distracting other students. Although teachers have tried providing Amelia with fidget tools to help her manage her energy and focus, the tools often end up broken due to using them inappropriately, like throwing them or using them in ways that are distracting to others. The frequency and intensity of Amelia's disruptive behaviors have escalated to the point where her teachers have sent her to the principal's office multiple times—a rare occurrence at Hilltop Elementary, where the staff prioritizes in-class behavior management strategies.

Amelia's disruptions not only affect her learning but also have a significant impact on the learning environment for her classmates. She has become a focal point for attention, making it difficult for her teachers to maintain a structured and focused classroom environment. Her classmates are often distracted by her actions, and some have begun to mimic her behavior. It has also been observed that many students who were once really friendly with her are not gravitating to her socially like they used to. The teaching staff recognizes that this behavior is beyond typical misbehavior and have expressed a desire for a comprehensive plan to address the root causes of Amelia's challenges.

Problem-Solving Approach

Recognizing that Amelia's behavior was not improving with basic classroom strategies, her homeroom teacher, Ms. Reed, reached out to the school's Student Support Team (SST) to discuss Amelia's behavior and seek guidance. The SST includes the school counselor, Dr. Whitman, the special education teacher, Ms. Carter, the school psychologist, Ms. Wells, and the school principal, Mr. James. The primary goal of the meeting was to identify underlying causes of Amelia's disruptive behavior and to develop an intervention plan that would help her regulate her behavior more effectively.

Ms. Reed also met with Amelia's parents, Mr. and Mrs. Brown, to gain a better understanding of her behavior at home. The parents reported that Amelia often struggled with focus and had difficulty following directions, particularly in situations where she was required to sit still or focus on one task for an extended period. They reported Amelia struggling with similar needs in after school activities as well. While they were aware of her fidgeting and high energy, they expressed concern that her behavior was becoming a barrier to her learning and social relationships. They were eager to work with the school to address Amelia's needs.

Team Collaboration

The SST meeting included the following team members:

1. **Ms. Reed (General Education Teacher):** Provided detailed observations of Amelia's behavior in the classroom and described the unsuccessful attempts to manage her disruptions with fidget tools and other strategies.

2. **Dr. Carter (Special Education Teacher):** Offered expertise in behavior management and suggested interventions tailored to Amelia's specific needs.

3. **Ms. Whitman (School Counselor):** Focused on understanding Amelia's emotional needs and helping her develop emotional regulation skills.
4. **Ms. Wells (School Psychologist):** Assisted in identifying any potential psychological factors contributing to Amelia's behavior and recommended evidence-based interventions.
5. **Mr. James (Principal):** Supported the team in coordinating resources and ensuring that the intervention plan could be implemented effectively school-wide.
6. **Mr. and Mrs. Brown (Parents):** Shared their perspective on Amelia's behavior at home and provided input on possible strategies that could work both at home and in school.

Designing the Intervention

The team identified several possible factors contributing to Amelia's behavior. These included difficulty with emotional regulation, sensory needs, and challenges with focusing during extended periods of instruction. They recognized that Amelia's disruptive behaviors were likely her way of communicating unmet needs, such as the need for movement, attention, or a different sensory input.

The team's primary goal was to design an intervention plan that would help Amelia replace her disruptive behaviors with more appropriate ways of getting her needs met. They also wanted to create a more structured environment that would support her focus and reduce the frequency of her trips to the principal's office.

Components of the Intervention

1. **Sensory Breaks and Movement Opportunities:**

    The team recognized that Amelia had a strong need for movement and sensory input. Instead of relying solely on fidget tools, which had not been effective for her, they implemented scheduled sensory breaks throughout the school day. Amelia would be allowed to take a short break to walk, stretch, or use a sensory corner equipped with a variety of sensory tools. Additionally, the team found a small table in storage that can be raised to a standing height. This table will be placed in the classroom as an option for any student who would prefer to stand while working.

2. **Behavior Replacement Plan:**

   Dr. Carter and Ms. Wells worked together to create a Behavior Replacement Plan (BRP) for Amelia. The BRP outlined specific replacement behaviors that Amelia could use instead of disrupting the class. For example, instead of shouting out during lessons, Amelia was taught to raise her hand when she wanted to speak. Additionally, when she felt restless, she could use a signal card to indicate that she needed a sensory break instead of getting out of her seat without permission. It was also determined that Amelia could get up at any time and use the standing table as a work space.

3. **Small Group Instruction:**

   Amelia often became most disruptive during whole-class instruction. To address this, Dr. Carter suggested that Amelia participate in small group instruction for certain subjects, such as math and reading. This smaller, more focused setting would provide her with more individualized attention and fewer distractions, helping her stay engaged and reducing her need to seek attention through disruptions. This was facilitated by Ms. Reed when students were tasked with independent or partner work during math or reading.

4. **Emotional Regulation Support:**

   Ms. Whitman began working with Amelia on emotional regulation skills. This included teaching her how to recognize when she was feeling frustrated or overwhelmed and providing strategies such as deep breathing exercises and positive self-talk to help her manage those feelings. Amelia was also given a "calm-down kit" to use when she felt the need for sensory input or a break. Amelia was added to Ms. Whitman's schedule once per week during the school wide intervention block.

Implementing the Interventions

With the intervention plan in place, Ms. Reed began implementing the strategies in her classroom. Amelia's day was structured to include sensory breaks at regular intervals, which allowed her to move and release energy in a controlled way. Ms. Reed introduced the signal card system to Amelia, explaining that she could use it to ask for a break instead of leaving her seat or disrupting the class.

Ms. Reed worked with Amelia in a small group setting during certain subjects, providing more targeted instruction and reducing distractions. This also included some re-teaching and pre-teaching of skills, while also targeting some social emotional skills through the academic process.

Ms. Whitman met with Amelia once a week to work on emotional regulation skills and to review her progress with using the calm-down kit and sensory breaks.

Personalized Support

The intervention plan was personalized to meet Amelia's specific needs for movement, sensory input, and emotional regulation. Ms. Reed provided frequent feedback to Amelia throughout the day, offering praise and encouragement when Amelia used the strategies that had been introduced. For example, when Amelia successfully used her signal card to request a break, Ms. Reed acknowledged her efforts with verbal praise, written praise, and non-verbal gestures.

Ms. Whitman provided individualized support during their small group sessions and emotional regulation meetings, ensuring that Amelia had the tools she needed to succeed.

Educating the Class

To continue building a supportive classroom environment, Ms. Reed held a class meeting to discuss emotions, behavior, and the importance of taking breaks. Without singling out Amelia, she explained that people have different ways of managing their feelings and energy levels, and it's important to respect each other's needs. The goal was to normalize the idea of taking breaks and using calming strategies so that Amelia's use of these tools would not be seen as unusual by her classmates. This was also the time that Ms. Reed introduced the standing table, having students model how it could be used and sharing that it was available for all students to try out and use.

The class meeting helped create a more understanding and empathetic classroom culture, which reduced the negative attention directed toward Amelia's behaviors.

Monitoring Progress

The SST regularly monitored Amelia's progress by collecting data on her behavior and engagement in class. Ms. Reed tracked the frequency of Amelia's disruptive behaviors, how often she used her signal card for breaks, and her overall positive participation in classroom activities and lessons. Ms. Whitman also gathered feedback from their sessions with Amelia, noting improvements in her emotional regulation and focus during small group work.

Initial Challenges

At first, Amelia had difficulty consistently using her signal card and sensory breaks. She often forgot to ask for a break when she felt restless and continued to get out of her seat without permission. The team realized that Amelia needed more direct reinforcement and reminders to help her adopt the new strategies. Additionally, Amelia initially struggled with the small group setting as she was used to receiving attention in larger, more disruptive ways.

Positive Developments

After several weeks of consistent implementation, Amelia began to show positive changes. She used her signal card more regularly to request breaks and became more engaged during small group instruction. The reward system proved to be an effective motivator, and Amelia started to look forward to earning points for appropriate behavior. Her disruptive outbursts and instances of leaving her seat without permission decreased, and she began using her sensory breaks more productively.

Amelia also demonstrated improvements in her emotional regulation skills. During one particularly challenging reading lesson, Amelia was observed taking deep breaths and using her calm-down kit to help her refocus, rather than disrupting the class.

Adjustments and Future Steps

Based on Amelia's progress, the team made several adjustments to the intervention plan. They increased the complexity of her tasks during small group instruction to keep her engaged and challenged. They also reduced the frequency of her sensory breaks as she showed greater ability to remain focused for longer periods.

The team also planned out a very simple reward system to encourage Amelia's use of strategies and her ability to self-manage her needs. At the start of the day, Amelia would choose what her reinforcer was from a bank of options. She typically chose stickers for her water bottle, but also liked to request a piece of stationary to write a note home to her parents about her day's successes. On Amelia's written daily schedule, she worked with Ms. Reed to put a star by the activities she was able to participate in with limited functional support. Each day a goal was set for the number of stars to receive her chosen reinforcer.

The team additionally decided that at the six-week mark, Amelia's reward system would be revisited to determine tweaks, how to reduce the need for tangible reinforcers, and to problem solve alongside Amelia to find a system that worked for everyone.

Continuous Support

The SST remained committed to providing continuous support for Amelia. Regular communication among Ms. Reed, Ms. Carter, Ms. Whitman, and Amelia's parents ensured that the strategies were reinforced both at school and at home. The team also planned to revisit Amelia's behavior plan periodically to make any necessary adjustments and ensure that she continued to make progress.

Conclusion

Amelia's case highlights the importance of a collaborative, individualized approach to addressing disruptive behavior in the classroom.

Through the combined efforts of her teachers, school staff, and parents, Amelia was able to develop the skills and strategies needed to manage her behavior and re-engage in learning. By providing structured support, positive reinforcement, and opportunities for movement and sensory input, the team helped Amelia replace her disruptive behaviors with more appropriate ways of expressing her needs. Through this, Amelia's classmates also were able to gain access to more universal ways of supporting movement and flexible seating. Offering these supports to all students extended the benefits and increased the likelihood of Amelia using the tools available in the classroom.

Although the process required patience and persistence, the positive changes in Amelia's behavior demonstrated the effectiveness of the intervention and the power of a supportive, tailored approach to managing disruptive behavior in young students. This case study serves as a reminder that with the right strategies, even the most challenging behaviors can be transformed into opportunities for growth and learning.

Case Study #2

Noah is a 6-year-old first-grade student at Oakwood Elementary School. Noah attended Oakwood Elementary School for kindergarten, where his year was pretty typical for kindergarten. Now that Noah is in first grade, he has been exhibiting highly disruptive behavior in the classroom on a daily basis. His teacher, Ms. Dawson, has noticed a consistent pattern of dysregulation beginning from the moment Noah arrives at school. Each morning, Noah has difficulty separating from his mother during drop-off, often clinging to her and becoming visibly upset when it is time for her to leave. This emotional dysregulation at the start of the day frequently spills over into the classroom, affecting Noah's behavior and ability to engage in learning.

Throughout the school day, Noah often blurts out loudly during lessons, interrupts his classmates, and engages in "class clown" behaviors, such as making jokes or funny faces to get a reaction from his peers. These behaviors not only disrupt the flow of instruction but also encourage other students to engage in off-task behavior, contributing to a chaotic classroom environment. Ms. Dawson has attempted various strategies, such as redirecting Noah and offering calming activities, but these efforts have not been successful in curbing his disruptive behavior.

Recognizing that Noah's difficulties with emotional regulation were beyond typical first-grade adjustment challenges, Ms. Dawson decided to seek additional support from the school's SST.

Problem-Solving Approach

Ms. Dawson brought her concerns to the SST, which included the school counselor, Ms. Thompson, the special education teacher, Mr. Ray, and the school psychologist, Dr. Green. The team discussed Noah's behaviors and the ways in which his morning separation difficulties were affecting his ability to regulate his emotions throughout the day. They also considered how Noah's desire to gain attention through class clown behaviors was likely linked to feelings of insecurity and anxiety.

To gain further insight, Ms. Dawson reached out to Noah's parents to discuss his behavior at home. Noah's mother confirmed that he often had difficulty with transitions and experienced separation anxiety in other situations, such as when being dropped off at playdates or activities. She also shared that Noah recently became a big brother and has struggled with the transition of having a baby in the home. His mom shared that Noah had a tendency to act out when he felt overwhelmed or unsure of himself, often using humor to deflect attention from his discomfort.

The goal of the SST meeting was to develop an intervention plan that would help Noah manage his emotions more effectively and reduce the frequency of his disruptive behaviors in the classroom.

Team Collaboration

The SST meeting included the following team members:

1. **Ms. Dawson (General Education 1st grade Teacher):** Provided observations of Noah's behavior in the 1st-grade classroom and detailed how his dysregulation after morning drop-off often escalated throughout the day.
2. **Mr. Ray (General Education Kindergarten Teacher):** Provided insights to Noah's kindergarten experience and any strategies or structures that seemed to benefit his participation in the classroom.
3. **Ms. Thompson (School Counselor):** Focused on strategies for addressing Noah's separation anxiety and helping him develop coping mechanisms for transitions.
4. **Dr. Green (School Psychologist):** Assisted in identifying potential underlying causes of Noah's behavior and recommended evidence-based interventions.
5. **Noah's Parents:** Shared their observations of Noah's behavior at home and collaborated on strategies to support Noah both at home and in school.

Designing the Intervention

After reviewing the information gathered from Noah's parents and discussing possible contributing factors to his behavior, the SST identified several key areas to target in its intervention plan:

1. **Separation Anxiety:** Noah's difficulty with separating from his mother each morning was a primary trigger for his dysregulation. The team needed to develop strategies to help Noah feel more secure and confident during morning drop-off.

2. **Emotional Regulation:** Noah's inability to regulate his emotions after becoming dysregulated in the morning often led to disruptive behavior throughout the day. The team aimed to teach Noah coping strategies to manage his emotions more effectively.

3. **Class Clown Behavior:** Noah's tendency to seek attention through disruptive and humorous behaviors was likely a way for him to mask feelings of insecurity or discomfort. The intervention would focus on providing Noah with positive ways to gain attention and build his self-esteem.

Components of the Intervention

The SST designed a multi-tiered intervention plan that addressed Noah's separation anxiety, emotional regulation, and attention-seeking behaviors.

1. **Morning Transition Support:**

    The team recognized that Noah needed a more structured and supportive transition into the school day to reduce his separation anxiety. Ms. Thompson, the school counselor, suggested creating a consistent morning routine that included a brief "goodbye ritual" with his mother and a calming activity immediately after drop-off. Noah's mother agreed to follow a set routine each morning, including a specific phrase they would use to say goodbye and a promise that she would return at the end of the day.

    Noah would also be assigned a "morning buddy," a trusted adult at school (Mr. Ray) who would meet him at the door each morning and walk him to the classroom. Since Mr. Ray has a classroom aide, it was determined that for four weeks, he could spend 3–4 minutes of the morning with Noah while his classroom aide supervised the kindergarten class. This would help Noah separate from his mother more smoothly and begin his day feeling supported.

2. **Emotional Regulation Strategies:**

   Noah needed to learn strategies to manage his emotions when he felt anxious or overwhelmed. Ms. Dawson and Ms. Thompson worked together to create a toolbox of emotional regulation techniques that Noah could try when he started to feel dysregulated. These included deep breathing exercises, using a stress ball, and taking short movement breaks when needed. With insight from Mr. Ray, the team learned that Noah is highly interested in outer space. The physical toolbox was created with an outer space theme including stars and stickers of planets and space ships to help encourage Noah to try the tools.

   Noah would also be given a space themed "calm-down card" that he could use to signal to Ms. Dawson when he needed a break. This card allowed Noah to step out of the classroom for a few minutes to reset, reducing the likelihood of him engaging in disruptive behavior. This also gave Noah some control and ownership over his strategies.

3. **Positive Reinforcement and Attention-Seeking Alternatives:**

   To address Noah's class clown behavior, the team worked on giving Noah positive attention in ways that reinforced appropriate behavior. For example, Ms. Dawson agreed to assign Noah small leadership roles in the classroom, such as being a line leader, passing out papers, and helping ring the classroom chime. This allowed Noah to gain attention in a constructive way and helped build his self-esteem.

Implementing the Intervention

With the intervention plan in place, Ms. Dawson and the SST began implementing the strategies in the classroom and during morning drop-off. Each morning, Mr. Ray met Noah at the door, greeting him with a cheerful, consistent routine. Noah and his mother followed the goodbye ritual they had practiced, and Noah was encouraged to engage in a calming activity, such as coloring or reading a book, before joining the rest of the class.

Ms. Thompson began meeting with Noah weekly for four weeks to practice emotional regulation strategies. They worked on deep breathing exercises, practiced using the calm-down card, and discussed ways Noah could recognize when he was feeling dysregulated. During these sessions, Noah also used role-play scenarios to practice handling situations where he might feel tempted to act out.

In the classroom, Ms. Dawson assigned Noah leadership roles, which allowed him to gain attention in a positive, structured way.

Personalized Support

The intervention was highly personalized to meet Noah's specific needs. Ms. Dawson provided frequent feedback to Noah throughout the day, offering praise and encouragement when he used his coping strategies effectively. For instance, when Noah successfully used his calm-down card to take a break instead of blurting out, Ms. Dawson praised him for making a positive choice and tied it directly to his job of being the line leader.

Ms. Thompson also provided personalized support, ensuring that Noah had access to the emotional regulation tools he needed throughout the day. They regularly checked in with him to discuss how he was feeling and reinforced the strategies they had practiced.

Educating the Class

To create a more supportive classroom environment, Ms. Dawson held a class meeting to discuss emotions and how everyone handles feelings differently. She explained that sometimes people need to take breaks to help themselves feel better and that this was a normal and healthy way to manage emotions. Without singling out Noah, she introduced the concept of using tools like calm-down cards and sensory tools to help stay focused and engaged.

This discussion helped normalize the idea of taking breaks and using coping strategies, which created a more understanding and empathetic classroom environment. Students became more aware of their own emotions and learned to respect each other's needs.

Monitoring Progress

The SST regularly monitored Noah's progress by tracking the frequency of his behavior in the classroom, noting how often he used his calm-down card and how frequently he engaged in disruptive behaviors. These data were shared weekly with Noah's parents to keep the lines of communication open between school and home. Ms. Thompson also met with Noah to review his progress in using emotional regulation strategies.

Initial Challenges

At first, Noah struggled to consistently use his calm-down card and emotional regulation tools. He continued to blurt out in class, and his desire for attention led to moments of class clown behavior despite the intervention. He also had difficulty transitioning smoothly from his mother in the mornings, and the goodbye ritual took longer than expected to have the desired calming effect.

The team realized that Noah needed more consistent reminders and reinforcement to help him adopt the new strategies. They increased the amount of immediate feedback he received and looped in all teachers (PE, art, drama, music, Mandarin) to ensure that offering positive feedback to Noah even for the smallest of wins was being prioritized.

Positive Developments

After several weeks of consistent implementation, Noah began to show positive changes. He started using his calm-down card more regularly to request breaks, and his class clown behavior decreased as he became more comfortable with gaining attention through positive leadership roles.

Noah also made progress in his morning transitions. While the separation from his mother was still difficult, the consistency of the goodbye ritual and the support from Mr. Ray helped Noah feel more secure as he entered the school building each day. After four weeks, the intervention of Mr. Ray's presence was slowly pulled away and Noah began joining a group of peers in line.

Adjustments and Future Steps

Based on Noah's progress, the team made several adjustments to the intervention plan. They gradually reduced the frequency of the breaks Noah could use daily as he showed greater ability to stay focused for longer periods. They also increased the complexity of his leadership roles in the classroom to continue building his confidence and self-esteem.

The team also discussed transitioning Noah's use of the calm-down card into a more internalized self-regulation strategy, gradually reducing the need for physical breaks as he developed stronger emotional regulation skills.

Continuous Support

The SST remained committed to providing continuous support for Noah. Regular communication between Ms. Dawson, Mr. Ray, Ms. Thompson, and Noah's parents ensured that the strategies were reinforced both at school and at home. The team planned to revisit Noah's behavior plan periodically to make any necessary adjustments and ensure his ongoing progress.

Conclusion

Noah's case demonstrates the importance of a collaborative, individualized approach to addressing disruptive behavior in young students. By working together, his teachers, school staff, and parents were able to create a comprehensive intervention plan that addressed the root causes of his behavior and provided him with the tools he needed to succeed.

Through consistent support, positive reinforcement, and opportunities for leadership, Noah began to develop the emotional regulation skills and self-confidence necessary to participate meaningfully in the classroom.

While the process required patience and persistence, the positive changes in Noah's behavior illustrate the effectiveness of the intervention and highlight the power of a supportive, structured approach to managing disruptive behavior.

CHAPTER SIX

Anxiety

ANXIETY IN students is a growing concern in schools today. Contrary to the misconception that anxiety is primarily an adult issue, it's so important to recognize that anxiety can deeply impact both children and adolescents. For students experiencing anxiety, the classroom can feel overwhelming, and their ability to engage and learn can be significantly compromised. Teachers and other school staff play a pivotal role in recognizing the signs of anxiety and creating an environment that supports students in overcoming these challenges, enabling them to thrive despite their struggles.

Recognizing Anxiety as a Barrier to Learning

Anxiety presents a unique set of challenges in the classroom because it's not always easy to spot. Unlike more outwardly disruptive behaviors, anxiety can be hidden behind quietness, avoidance, perfectionism, or even excessive compliance. Dr. Lori Desautels emphasizes that anxiety can wreak havoc and dysregulate the nervous system, making it difficult for students to engage with learning in a meaningful way. When students are in a state of emotional dysregulation due to anxiety, their brain's ability to process information, think critically, or problem-solve can be significantly impaired. When we consider this impact, it shows how tricky it can be to accurately assess children on their academic knowledge who are also experiencing high levels of anxiety. Perhaps they are exceptionally stressed regarding the assessment, or maybe they were unable to attend to the instruction previously in order to comprehend the content they're even being assessed on.

Dr. Marc Brackett reinforces the idea that emotions play a critical role in how we engage with learning. When anxiety is present, it can act as a barrier, causing students to withdraw, shut down, or disengage entirely. Recognizing that anxiety is not just a "side issue" but a core obstacle to learning is the first step in creating a supportive classroom for students who experience it.

A critical piece of this puzzle is acknowledging that students may not always express their anxiety in obvious ways. Some students may become hyper-focused on avoiding failure, while others might act out in frustration because they feel overwhelmed. Anxiety often manifests differently in every person affected, and being attuned to these signs is key to offering the right support.

Common Manifestations of Anxiety in the Classroom

As we've said, anxiety can show up in different ways depending on the student. Some students may be visibly anxious, while others may internalize their struggles. Here are a few common ways anxiety might manifest in the classroom:

- Perfectionism: Students may work slowly or avoid completing tasks out of fear that their work won't be "good enough."

- Frequent bathroom breaks or illness: Students with anxiety often ask to leave the room frequently or complain of physical symptoms like stomach aches or headaches. This also may be students who are continually heading to the nurse's office.

- Avoidance: Some students may avoid certain subjects, social interactions, or activities that trigger their anxiety.
- Excessive compliance or withdrawn behavior: Highly anxious students may appear overly compliant, not wanting to make any mistakes or stand out. On the flip side, they may become silent, avoiding participation altogether.
- Outbursts or defiance: Anxiety doesn't always look like worry. For some students, anxiety can lead to emotional outbursts or defiant behavior as a response to overwhelming feelings.

Dr. Bruce Perry points out that anxiety can be deeply tied to a student's past experiences or current stressors. Whether it's due to instability at home, social struggles, or academic pressure, anxiety can create a "fight, flight, or freeze" response in students, disrupting their ability to learn and participate effectively in class. Perry explains that when students feel unsafe or unsure in their environment, their brain's survival instincts take over, making it difficult to focus on anything else. This means that for students grappling with anxiety, even simple tasks can feel monumental.

Addressing Anxiety in the Classroom

Once we recognize that anxiety is a barrier to learning, the next step is developing strategies to support students who are struggling. The good news is there are many proactive strategies we can implement that benefit not just our anxious students but all learners in our classroom. Dr. Dan Siegel reminds us that building a sense of safety and connection in the classroom helps regulate students' emotional states, allowing them to engage more fully in learning. This Tier 1 approach makes your classroom anxiety friendly, knowing that anxiety may be a hidden struggle for some students.

Here are simple, research-backed strategies to support students with anxiety.

Stay Structured

Structure and predictability are essential for students with anxiety. As we can assume, anxious students often feel a sense of uncertainty about their day. A well-organized classroom with clear, consistent routines can provide much-needed stability. Posting a daily schedule that includes visuals and written words helps students anticipate what's coming next and can reduce the anxiety that stems from uncertainty.

Students experiencing anxiety often struggle with the unknown. Something as simple as a surprise change in the day's schedule can send an anxious student into a spiral of worry and "what if's." A structured environment, where they can visually see what's coming next, helps to alleviate this sense of unpredictability. For students who need extra support, providing individual schedules can be a great tool. These individualized schedules give anxious students something concrete to rely on, which can help them feel more secure.

Create Designated Calm Spaces

Dr. Lori Desautels talks about the importance of "brain breaks" and calm spaces in the classroom. Calm corners aren't just for students with visible anger issues; they can be a refuge for students feeling overwhelmed. A universal space in the classroom where students can retreat to when they're feeling big emotions can make the entire environment feel safer. This space can include sensory tools, calming visuals, and quiet activities that help students self-regulate before rejoining the class.

Creating a safe, calming area in your classroom signals to students that it's okay to take a break when they're feeling anxious. These spaces provide an opportunity for students to reset emotionally before returning to their work. For some students, even a few minutes in this space can prevent a complete emotional shutdown.

Affirmations: Counteracting Negative Thoughts

For many students, anxiety manifests as an internal dialogue full of negative self-talk. Their anxious brain can act like a hamster wheel, constantly repeating thoughts like "I'm not good enough," "I can't do this," or "Everyone's judging me." Introducing positive affirmations in the classroom can help break that cycle. By giving students daily reminders that they are capable, valued, and strong, we can start to shift their inner narrative.

Visual tools like affirmation cards or coloring journals can be especially powerful. Encouraging students to choose or create their own positive mantras helps them internalize these affirmations and use them as a coping strategy when anxiety flares up. Affirmation cards can be a structured way to support students in building this strategy.

Breathing Exercises

Breathing exercises are one of the most straightforward and effective ways to help students manage anxiety in real-time. Dr. Nadine Burke-Harris, a pediatrician and expert on adverse childhood experiences, highlights the role of mindfulness and breathing in calming the nervous system. Making breathing exercises an intentional part of the classroom routine can be a lifesaver for students who experience anxiety.

There are a variety of breathing strategies, ranging from simple deep breaths to more complex techniques like box breathing (inhale for four counts, hold for four, exhale for four, hold for four). Teaching these exercises proactively helps students feel equipped to use them when anxiety hits. Integrating these practices into your classroom doesn't just help the anxious students—it creates a calmer, more focused learning environment for everyone.

These shape breathing mats can structure this in a way that makes it more concrete and less lofty for students who require that additional support. Access them through the QR code below.

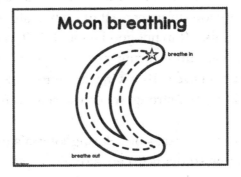

Movement and Exercise: Endorphins to Combat Anxiety

Dr. Bruce Perry's research reminds us that movement is not just good for physical health—it's a crucial component of mental well-being. Movement releases endorphins, which help reduce anxiety. Incorporating movement into daily lessons, offering short physical breaks, or scheduling time for activities like guided stretches or movement videos can provide anxious students with a much-needed release.

For students who struggle with sitting still due to anxiety, even small movement breaks—like walking across the room to get a drink of water or doing a few jumping jacks—can help them reset and refocus. Having a tall table available as a standing work option or offering a spot where students can pace during instruction can be the small tweak that makes the biggest difference. The goal here is to provide students with outlets for their anxious energy without disrupting the learning environment.

Regular Check-Ins: Building Connection

Anxiety can make students feel isolated and misunderstood. Scheduling intentional check-in times can offer anxious students an opportunity to vent, ask questions, and gain reassurance. Dr. Marc Brackett advocates for building strong, trusting relationships with students to support their emotional well-being. These 1:1 check-ins don't have to be long, but they can go a long way in helping students feel seen and supported.

Check-ins can be informal or scheduled into the day, but the key is consistency. Knowing they'll have a chance to talk about their feelings with a trusted adult can alleviate much of the pressure that anxiety builds over the course of the school day.

Adding in an adult check-in additionally adds another adult to their trusted circle. Dr. Bruce Perry reminds us that "relationships are the agents of change," and the more meaningful relationships we can add to a child's life and daily routine, the better.

> "Relationships are the agents of change."
> —Dr. Bruce Perry

Accommodations: Flexibility Is Key

Students with anxiety may need accommodations to feel comfortable and supported in the classroom. This might mean giving them extra wait time, offering additional prompts, or allowing more space when they're feeling overwhelmed. For some students, accommodations like extended time on assignments or tests can alleviate the pressure that triggers anxiety.

As Dr. Ross Greene reminds us, being flexible with anxious students doesn't mean lowering expectations—it means providing the right supports so they can meet those expectations. By offering accommodations that meet their needs, we're setting them up for success rather than setting them up for stress.

Positive Distractions to Break the Anxiety Cycle

Sometimes, anxious thoughts can become so pervasive that they take over. Providing students with positive distractions can help break the cycle of worry and bring their focus back to the present. Sensory tools like stress balls or simple puzzles can give students something else to focus on when their anxiety is high.

For younger students, quiet activities like coloring, reading calming books, or a simple matching activity can help calm their thoughts and regain their sense of control.

Bibliotherapy: Learning Through Stories

Books have the power to teach us new skills and show us that we're not alone. Bibliotherapy—using books to help students understand and cope with anxiety—can be a powerful tool in the classroom. There are many books designed for children that explore themes of anxiety, fear, and coping strategies.

Reading these books aloud or incorporating them into lessons can help students see their own experiences reflected in the characters, which can reduce feelings of isolation.

Explicitly Teach Coping Skills

Coping skills aren't one-size-fits-all. Teaching a variety of coping skills gives students the opportunity to experiment and find out what works for them. For some, deep breathing will be the answer. For others, physical movement, creative outlets, or talking to a trusted adult may be more effective.

Giving students a "toolbox" of coping skills equips them with strategies they can use both inside and outside of school. This helps students feel empowered and in control, even when their anxiety rears its head.

Creating an Anxiety-Friendly Classroom

Students with anxiety face unique challenges, but with the right supports, they can thrive in the classroom. By recognizing the signs of anxiety and implementing strategies like calm spaces, positive affirmations, and mindfulness practices, teachers can create an environment that supports students' emotional well-being.

It's important to remember that anxiety is not a sign of weakness or defiance. It's a very real, very human experience that many of our students are navigating daily. With empathy, flexibility, and a toolkit of proactive strategies, we can create a classroom that not only acknowledges anxiety but helps students manage it, allowing them to fully engage in learning.

Case Study #1

Dinasia, an 8-year-old third-grade student at Crow Elementary School. Dinasia loves animals, being a big sister, and watching shows on YouTube. This school year, Dinasia has been exhibiting significant anxiety in the classroom, primarily centered around her need for perfection in both academic and creative tasks. She has developed a pattern of crying at least once a day, usually during her attempts to complete academic assignments or during art class, where her desire for precision becomes overwhelming. Dinasia's perfectionism manifests in her reluctance to make mistakes, and she often tears up her work if it does not meet her own high standards. She has a particular fear of making mistakes in math, spelling, and drawing.

Her teacher, Mrs. Taylor, first noticed Dinasia's tendency to freeze when faced with difficult tasks early in the school year. During a math lesson, Dinasia became visibly distressed when she made a mistake on a worksheet, crying and crumpling up the paper. Since then, Dinasia's crying episodes have increased in frequency, becoming a daily occurrence. Mrs. Taylor also observed that when Dinasia struggles, she will avoid completing assignments, claiming, "I can't do it right," or asking for constant reassurance and direction. These behaviors often leave Dinasia feeling overwhelmed and frustrated, and her peers are beginning to notice, which only adds to her stress.

Problem Solving Approach

After noticing the consistent emotional struggles, Mrs. Taylor contacted Dinasia's parents to better understand whether these behaviors were present at home. Dinasia's mother shared that she has always been highly sensitive, especially when it comes to schoolwork and creative projects. Both of Dinasia's parents attended Ivy League universities and are doctors at the local hospital. Academics have been highly encouraged in their home with all of their children. Dinasia's mom reports that Dinasia becomes upset if her homework is not "perfect" and will often cry during family activities that require creativity, like drawing or crafting. Both parents mentioned that they are aware of Dinasia's anxiety and have been providing emotional support, but they were unsure of how to manage it effectively.

Recognizing that Dinasia's behavior was becoming a significant barrier to her learning, Mrs. Taylor initiated a conversation with the school counselor, Mr. Johnson. He agreed that Dinasia's anxiety warranted a targeted intervention plan to help her manage her perfectionism and develop healthier coping mechanisms.

Team Collaboration

1. **Mrs. Taylor (3rd-grade teacher):** Focused on classroom strategies and implementing them across the classroom.
2. **Mr. Johnson (School Counselor):** Worked with Dinasia on emotional regulation and coping skills.
3. **Dr. Parker (School psychologist):** Provided administrative support as well as clinical expertise on anxiety and how it may affect academics and overall school performance.
4. **Mr. and Mrs. Griffin (parents):** Provided insights to home experiences and ways to carry over interventions after school hours.

During the meeting, the team discussed Dinasia's academic and social performance, her emotional regulation challenges, and potential triggers for her anxiety. Mrs. Taylor noted that Dinasia was academically capable but often struggled to complete tasks due to her fear of making mistakes. Dr. Parker, who had observed Dinasia during small group sessions, agreed that she appeared highly capable but that her anxiety significantly hindered her ability to demonstrate her knowledge.

Dr. Parker explained that perfectionism often stems from underlying anxiety and can be rooted in a fear of failure. She suggested that Dinasia's intense emotional responses were likely due to a heightened fear of judgment, either from herself or others, and that her tears were her way of releasing the built-up emotional tension from these fears.

Designing the Intervention

With this understanding, the team agreed to focus the intervention on helping Dinasia develop resilience, manage her anxiety, and reduce her perfectionistic tendencies. They decided to implement a multi-tiered intervention that included strategies to address both the emotional and academic aspects of her perfectionism.

Key components of the intervention included:

1. **Emotional Regulation Strategies:** Dinasia needed tools to help her manage her emotional response to perceived failure. The team decided to introduce her to mindfulness and breathing exercises that she could use when she began to feel overwhelmed. The school counselor, Mr. Johnson, would lead a series of weekly small-group sessions focusing on emotional regulation, specifically for students experiencing anxiety.

2. **Growth Mindset Development:** To shift Dinasia's mindset away from perfectionism, the intervention would include a focus on promoting a growth mindset. Mrs. Taylor would integrate positive self-talk, growth mindset language, and discussions about the value of mistakes into the classroom culture. The goal was to help Dinasia and her peers understand that mistakes are part of the learning process.

3. **Coping Skills Toolbox:** Dinasia would be provided with a personalized "coping skills toolbox" that included visual reminders of strategies she could use when feeling anxious. This toolbox would include affirmation cards, a stress ball, a set of colored pencils for coloring provided mandala coloring pages, and a list of positive coping phrases.

4. **Flexible Assignments and Modified Expectations:** To alleviate some of the pressure Dinasia placed on herself, Mrs. Taylor would provide her with modified assignments when necessary. For example, instead of requiring Dinasia to complete an entire worksheet without errors, the teacher would allow her to focus on completing

three to five problems to the best of her ability. Art projects would be less structured, allowing Dinasia to express creativity without the expectation of perfection.

Components of the Intervention

The intervention had four key components:

1. **Mindfulness and Breathing Techniques:** To help Dinasia manage her anxiety in the moment, the team taught her simple breathing exercises like deep belly breaths and the "5-4-3-2-1 grounding technique."

5-4-3-2-1 Ground Technique

The 5-4-3-2-1 grounding technique is a practical mindfulness strategy that helps students manage feelings of stress, anxiety, or frustration by anchoring them in the present moment. It guides students to focus on their senses, starting with 5 things they can see, 4 things they can touch, 3 things they can hear, 2 things they can smell, and 1 thing they can taste. By engaging their senses, students redirect their attention from overwhelming emotions to their immediate environment, promoting calmness and self-regulation. This technique is simple, adaptable, and effective for students of all ages in building emotional awareness and resilience.

Dinasia was encouraged to use these techniques when she felt overwhelmed or anxious about a task. Mrs. Taylor also taught this technique to the class during Morning Meeting, and prompted its use throughout the day to reinforce and practice.

5-4-3-2-1 Grounding technique

A calming technique that connects you with the present by exploring the five senses.

Directions: Sitting or standing, take a deep breath in, and answer the questions below.

5 — 5 things you can see

4 — 4 things you can touch

3 — 3 things you can hear

2 — 2 things you can smell

1 — 1 thing you can taste

2. **Growth Mindset Lessons:** Mrs. Taylor began teaching explicit lessons on growth mindset, incorporating children's books that promoted the message that mistakes are opportunities for growth. The class began using phrases such as, "Mistakes help me learn" and "I can keep trying even if it's hard."

3. **Gradual Exposure to Mistakes:** To help Dinasia reduce her fear of making mistakes, the team implemented a strategy where she would gradually face tasks that involved small, intentional mistakes. For example, in art class, she was encouraged to start projects without the expectation that they would be perfect. Initially, she was provided with small, manageable drawing tasks with the understanding that "imperfection is okay."

4. **Coping Skills Toolbox:** Dinasia's personalized toolbox was introduced, and she was taught how to use each item effectively. The toolbox became a source of comfort, and Dinasia could reach for it during challenging moments.

Implementing the Intervention

Once the intervention plan was finalized, the team began implementation. Mr. Johnson started meeting with Dinasia in small groups once a week, where they practiced mindfulness exercises and discussed coping strategies for anxiety. Dinasia responded well to these sessions, as they provided her with a safe space to express her feelings.

In the classroom, Mrs. Taylor introduced growth mindset lessons to the whole class, using books and discussions to normalize making mistakes. The classroom environment began to shift, with students learning to embrace challenges rather than fear them. This was evidenced by students reminding one another of the value in mistakes, and less students complaining or verbally announcing frustration over mistakes.

At the same time, Dinasia was encouraged to use her coping skills toolbox whenever she felt anxious. Mrs. Taylor provided regular positive reinforcement when Dinasia used these tools, praising her for taking steps to manage her emotions.

Personalized Support

Dinasia's parents were also involved in the intervention process. At home, they reinforced the growth mindset concepts Dinasia was learning in school. They worked with her on assignments and projects, focusing less on the outcome and more on the effort she put into the task. Her parents shared their family pride in their academic and professional accomplishments, and began sharing other personal stories with Dinasia about how certain mistakes or "bumps in the road" actually helped them along the way.

Additionally, the school psychologist, Dr. Parker, conducted two individual sessions with Dinasia to help her identify specific triggers for her anxiety. These sessions provided more personalized insights into Dinasia's thought processes, which helped inform the ongoing intervention.

Educating the Class

One key aspect of the intervention was educating Dinasia's peers about anxiety and perfectionism in an age-appropriate way. Mrs. Taylor facilitated class discussions about feelings, mistakes, and how everyone has different strengths and challenges. The goal was to create a supportive, inclusive classroom environment where students felt comfortable expressing their emotions and taking academic risks.

These discussions not only helped Dinasia feel more supported but also reduced any stigma around her emotional outbursts. As students learned about growth mindset and the normalcy of mistakes, they became more empathetic and less judgmental toward one another.

Monitoring Progress

The team closely monitored Dinasia's progress over the following weeks. Mrs. Taylor kept track of the number of crying incidents, noting whether they were decreasing in frequency and intensity. Dinasia's use of her coping toolbox was also tracked, as was her engagement in classwork.

The school counselor, Mr. Johnson, met with Dinasia weekly to check in on her emotional state and assess her progress in managing her anxiety. These meetings provided Dinasia with a safe space to reflect on her emotions and practice the skills she was learning.

Initial Challenges

During the first few weeks of the intervention, Dinasia showed some resistance. Although she understood the growth mindset concepts, she still had difficulty accepting mistakes, particularly in art class. At times, she would revert to crying when her drawing didn't look "just right" and even making holes in her papers from the amount of erasing she was doing.

Mrs. Taylor also noticed that Dinasia was hesitant to use her coping toolbox in front of her peers. She shared that she feared that it would draw attention to her anxiety, which exacerbated her feelings of self-consciousness.

Positive Developments

As the weeks progressed, however, Dinasia began to show small signs of improvement. By the end of the second month, Dinasia's crying incidents had decreased from daily to every few days. She also started using her breathing techniques more regularly, particularly during math lessons, where it was found that her anxiety was highest.

One of the biggest turning points came during an art lesson, where Dinasia completed a drawing and proudly showed it to Mrs. Taylor even though it wasn't perfect by her previous standards. Dinasia acknowledged, "It's not exactly how I wanted, but I like how it turned out." This was a major step forward in reducing her perfectionistic tendencies.

Adjustments and Future Steps

After seeing the initial progress, the team adjusted the intervention slightly. They added more frequent check-ins with Mr. Johnson, and modified the math curriculum to include more collaborative problem-solving, which allowed Dinasia to feel supported by her peers rather than isolated in her struggle.

Continuous Support

Dinasia's progress was celebrated, but the team recognized that anxiety and perfectionism are ongoing challenges that require continuous support. They decided to keep the intervention in place for the remainder of the school year, with regular check-ins to monitor her emotional well-being and academic performance.

Dinasia's parents were encouraged to continue reinforcing the growth mindset strategies at home, and they agreed to meet with the team at the end of the year to assess whether further interventions or supports would be necessary moving forward.

Conclusion

Dinasia's case highlights the complex interaction between anxiety, perfectionism, and learning. By working collaboratively, Dinasia's teachers, parents, and support staff were able to create a personalized intervention that helped her develop emotional regulation strategies and reduce her reliance on perfectionism. While challenges remain, Dinasia's progress is a testament to the power of targeted interventions, growth mindset development, and emotional support in helping students overcome significant anxiety and thrive in the classroom.

Case Study #2

Edwin is a 9-year-old 4th-grade student at Valley View Tech Elementary. Edwin is very involved in his church's youth group, loves soccer, and is bilingual in Spanish and English. It's been noted throughout Edwin's school experience at Valley View Tech that he has always had notable anxiety. This year, he has been struggling with significant anxiety that affects nearly every aspect of his school life. His anxiety manifests in many ways, from hiding under tables or in his locker during stressful moments to avoiding social interactions with his peers. Over the summer, Edwin was in a small car accident while riding with his grandfather. Although no one was injured, the incident significantly heightened his already present anxiety, triggering a host of new fears, particularly around loud noises, sudden transitions, and weather-related events.

Edwin's anxiety is pervasive, leading him to constantly worry with "what if?" thoughts such as, "What if it starts storming?" or "What if something bad happens?" These fears make it difficult for him to focus on his schoolwork, form friendships, or engage in typical classroom activities. His general education teacher, Ms. Hayes, noticed as early as the first day of school that Edwin often avoids class participation and will retreat to the bathroom for long periods of time when he feels overwhelmed. His anxiety not only affects his academic progress but also impairs his ability to form and maintain social relationships with his peers, who are beginning to notice his frequent absences from class and unusual behavior.

After the car accident, Edwin's parents sought help from an outside pediatric therapist, Dr. Roberts, to provide additional support for his anxiety. While Edwin had always shown signs of anxiety, the accident intensified his fears, prompting the need for specialized therapeutic intervention outside of school.

Problem-Solving Approach

Ms. Hayes first observed Edwin's heightened anxiety during the initial weeks of the school year, which was about a month after he experienced the car accident. During an unexpected fire drill, Edwin panicked and bolted from the classroom, hiding in his locker. Ms. Hayes tried to coax him out, but Edwin remained in the locker for over 20 minutes, visibly shaking and crying. Concerned about his well-being, Ms. Hayes reached out to the school's social worker, Ms. Lee, for additional support.

Ms. Hayes and Ms. Lee began documenting Edwin's behavior, particularly around loud noises, transitions between activities, and weather-related events. They noted that Edwin's anxiety seemed to spike during recess and outdoor activities, especially if the weather was cloudy or windy. Additionally, Edwin had begun avoiding peer interactions, preferring to sit alone during group activities or free time.

During a conversation with Edwin's parents, they confirmed that Edwin's anxiety had worsened since the accident. His mother explained that Edwin frequently experienced "what if?" thoughts and required constant reassurance at home. She also mentioned that they had recently started taking Edwin to Dr. Roberts, a pediatric therapist specializing in childhood anxiety, to help him develop coping skills and plan as a family how to move forward effectively.

Recognizing the need for a comprehensive approach, Ms. Lee suggested reaching out to Dr. Roberts to ensure consistency between Edwin's therapy sessions and the support he received at school. Edwin's parents signed a release form, allowing communication between the school team and Dr. Roberts.

Team Collaboration

A collaborative team was assembled to create a support plan for Edwin. This team included:

Ms. Hayes (General Education Teacher): Focused on classroom strategies to help Edwin manage his anxiety throughout the school day.

Ms. Lee (School Social Worker): Provided emotional and social support for Edwin, helping him address his underlying anxiety and fears.

Mr. Thompson (School Psychologist): Assisted with understanding the psychological aspects of Edwin's anxiety and how they related to his behavior in school.

Ms. Rivera (Special Education Coordinator): Provided insights on behavior interventions and accommodations that could support Edwin within the general education environment.

Edwin's Parents: Actively participated in the planning process, sharing insights into Edwin's behavior at home and coordinating his therapy with the school team.

Dr. Roberts (Pediatric Therapist): Collaborated with the school team to align therapeutic goals and provide feedback on Edwin's progress.

Dr. Roberts requested specific data collection from the school team to better understand how Edwin's anxiety was showing up in the classroom. She asked Ms. Hayes to document the frequency, duration, and triggers of Edwin's anxious behaviors, particularly his tendencies to hide in his locker, avoid social interactions, or retreat to the bathroom. This data would help Dr. Roberts tailor Edwin's therapy sessions to address the situations he faced at school.

The team agreed to share regular updates with Dr. Roberts, providing her with detailed observations about Edwin's behavior. In turn, Dr. Roberts would offer suggestions for additional coping strategies and techniques to be implemented in the classroom.

Designing the Intervention

With input from Dr. Roberts and the school team's observations, a personalized intervention plan was developed to help Edwin manage his anxiety. The plan addressed both his emotional and social challenges, with a focus on equipping Edwin with tools to handle his fears more effectively.

Key components of the intervention included:

1. **Coping Skills for Anxiety Management:** Ms. Lee and Dr. Roberts collaborated to teach Edwin coping strategies, such as deep breathing exercises, grounding techniques, and positive self-talk. These skills would help Edwin regulate his anxiety during loud noises, transitions, or weather-related triggers.

2. **Relaxation Space:** A designated calm-down space would be created in Ms. Hayes' classroom where Edwin could retreat when feeling overwhelmed. The space would include sensory tools like stress balls, calming visuals, noise reducing headphones, and a weighted blanket to help Edwin self-regulate without needing to leave the classroom.

3. **Social Skills Support:** Edwin's anxiety had impacted his friendships, so the intervention included social skills support. Ms. Lee would work with Edwin in small group settings to practice engaging with peers and rebuilding his confidence in social interactions.

4. **Classroom Accommodations:** Edwin would be given additional time to transition between activities, and Ms. Hayes would provide advance warnings about any upcoming loud noises, such as fire drills. Edwin would also have access to noise-reducing headphones during particularly loud or overwhelming moments.

5. **Communication Between School and Therapist:** The school team would provide regular data on Edwin's behaviors to Dr. Roberts, who would offer feedback on Edwin's progress and suggest adjustments to the intervention plan. This collaboration ensured that Edwin's school and therapy experiences were aligned and mutually supportive.

Components of the Intervention

The intervention was structured around Edwin's specific triggers and needs. The components included:

1. **Mindfulness and Breathing Techniques:** Ms. Lee introduced Edwin to simple breathing exercises, such as "balloon breathing" (pretending to blow up a balloon by taking deep breaths) and the "5-4-3-2-1" grounding technique, which focuses on using the senses to bring attention back to the present moment. Edwin practiced these techniques during class when he felt anxious, and Ms. Hayes reinforced their use in the classroom.

2. **Personalized Check-Ins:** Ms. Hayes scheduled daily check-ins with Edwin to provide emotional reassurance and gauge how he was feeling. These brief moments of connection helped Edwin feel supported and gave Ms. Hayes the opportunity to address any immediate concerns before they escalated.

3. **Relaxation Space:** A calm-down corner was set up in Ms. Hayes' classroom, equipped with sensory tools, calming coloring pages, and a visual timer. Edwin was encouraged to use the space when needed, allowing him to self-regulate without needing to leave the room entirely.

4. **Social Skills Group:** Ms. Lee created a small social skills group that met once a week to help Edwin practice social interactions in a safe environment. The group engaged in cooperative games, role-playing, and discussions about building friendships, providing Edwin with a supportive space to rebuild his confidence in peer interactions.

Implementing the Intervention

Once the intervention plan was finalized, the team began implementation. Ms. Hayes created a more predictable classroom environment, giving Edwin advance notice of transitions and any potentially loud activities. Fire drills, which previously caused Edwin intense anxiety, were preempted with discussions about what to expect, and Edwin and any other student had access to noise-reducing headphones to use during the drill.

Ms. Lee met with Edwin twice a week for 20-minute sessions where they practiced mindfulness, breathing techniques, and self-regulation strategies. Edwin also used these sessions to discuss his fears, particularly those related to weather and loud noises. Together, they worked on "what if?" scenarios, helping Edwin challenge his anxious thoughts with more realistic possibilities.

The relaxation corner in Ms. Hayes' classroom became a valuable resource for Edwin. Initially, he continued to leave the classroom, but over time, he became more accustomed to retreating to the corner when feeling anxious, rather than leaving the classroom space altogether.

The team began collecting data on Edwin's use of the relaxation corner, his participation in class activities, and the frequency and duration of his more outward anxious behaviors. These data were shared with Dr. Roberts, who used it to adjust Edwin's therapy sessions and provide feedback to the school team.

Personalized Support

Edwin's parents played a critical role in reinforcing the strategies he was learning at school. At home, they practiced the same breathing exercises and grounding techniques that Edwin was using in class, helping to create consistency between home and school.

Dr. Roberts remained in close communication with the school team, reviewing the data collected by Ms. Hayes and Ms. Lee. This collaboration allowed Dr. Roberts to adjust Edwin's therapy goals and provide recommendations for additional supports, such as introducing visual aids to help Edwin track his progress and manage his anxiety.

Educating the Class

Ms. Hayes recognized the importance of creating a classroom environment where Edwin felt more understood, heard, and accepted by his peers. She held class discussions about anxiety and how everyone experiences fear differently. These conversations were designed to normalize anxiety and create a culture of empathy in the classroom.

Ms. Hayes also introduced mindfulness practices to the whole class, teaching students breathing exercises and relaxation techniques. This benefited not only Edwin but also the entire class, helping to reduce stress and foster a more supportive learning environment.

The relaxation corner was also opened up for the entire class of students, sharing that, since all people experience a wide range of big emotions, it makes sense that it would be a place that anyone could use when needed.

Monitoring Progress

The team monitored Edwin's progress closely, keeping track of his use of the relaxation corner and his participation in social skills group. Data were shared regularly with Dr. Roberts, who used it to assess Edwin's emotional state and make adjustments to his therapy sessions.

Initial Challenges

Initially, Edwin's behavior didn't seem to change. While he was a part of the whole class discussions regarding coping skills, it did not always appear that Edwin was making connections to his own experiences. He also hesitated to use the relaxation corner in front of his peers and continued to leave the classroom. Socially, Edwin remained quiet and reserved in the social skills group, avoiding direct interaction with his peers.

Positive Developments

Despite the initial challenges, Edwin began to make gradual improvements. He started using the relaxation corner more frequently and reduced his time spent hiding in the locker or bathroom. Edwin's participation in the social skills group also improved, and he began contributing to discussions and engaging in cooperative activities with his peers.

During a particularly windy day, which would have previously caused Edwin to retreat to the bathroom, he was able to stay in the classroom and use his noise-reducing headphones. This marked a major turning point in his ability to cope with anxiety.

Adjustments and Future Steps

After observing Edwin's progress, the team made several adjustments to the intervention. They introduced a visual schedule to help Edwin anticipate transitions and feel more in control of his day. Ms. Hayes also increased Edwin's participation in group activities, encouraging him to take on small roles in class projects.

The social skills group was expanded to include more structured activities that allowed Edwin to practice interacting with peers in a controlled setting. He continued to receive regular check-ins from Ms. Lee to ensure Edwin felt supported.

Continuous Support

Recognizing that Edwin's anxiety would be an ongoing challenge, the team committed to providing continuous support. Edwin's intervention plan would remain in place for the rest of the school year, with regular reviews and adjustments as needed.

Dr. Roberts and the school team maintained open communication to ensure that Edwin's therapy and school supports remained aligned. Edwin's parents continued to reinforce the strategies at home, helping him build resilience and manage his anxiety in both settings.

Edwin's parents shared with the school team that Dr. Roberts had suggested anti-anxiety medication.

Conclusion

Edwin's case shows us how complex childhood anxiety can really be. It also highlights the importance of taking a collaborative, multidisciplinary approach. Through the combined efforts of his teachers, school social worker, parents, and outside therapist, Edwin was able to develop coping strategies that helped him manage his fears and engage more fully in school. While challenges may always remain for Edwin, his progress illustrates for us the tremendous value of targeted interventions, personalized support, and ongoing collaboration in helping students with significant anxiety succeed in the classroom.

CHAPTER SEVEN

Aggression

I'M GOING to make an assumption that we have all been there—dealing with a student whose aggression in the classroom feels like it's throwing the entire day off course. It's one of the hardest behaviors to manage, not just because of the disruption but because of the emotional toll it takes on everyone involved. When a student is yelling, hitting, throwing objects, or intimidating others, it's easy to feel frustrated and overwhelmed. And the truth is, managing aggression can be exhausting. But behind every act of aggression is a story, often a complex one, and our job as educators is to figure out what's fueling that behavior and how to help the student work through it.

Aggression isn't just a "discipline issue"—it's a barrier to learning. It creates a wall between students and their ability to engage with school, and it can leave their classmates feeling unsafe, distracted, or anxious. Our goal isn't just to stop the aggressive behavior; it's to get to the root of the problem, build trust, and help students develop healthier ways to cope. So let's take a deep breath and dive into understanding why aggression happens, what triggers it, and, most importantly, what we can do about it.

Recognizing Aggression as a Barrier to Learning and Engagement

Aggressive behavior can look different depending on the student and the situation. It might show up as yelling, hitting, kicking, or throwing things. Maybe it's more verbal aggression, like name-calling or threats. Or maybe it's more subtle, like intimidating peers or engaging in disruptive behavior that keeps the whole class from moving forward. No matter how aggression manifests, it is a huge obstacle to learning.

When students are aggressive, they're not just making things difficult for their teachers and classmates. They're also making things harder for themselves. They can't focus on their schoolwork, they're often in trouble, and their relationships with peers and adults become strained. Dr. Bruce Perry explains that when kids are in a state of high emotional arousal (like anger or fear), their brain isn't focused on learning. Instead, it's in survival mode—fight, flight, or freeze—which means they're not absorbing information or engaging with what's happening around them.

It's important to remember that aggressive behavior is often a symptom of something deeper. Dr. Lori Desautels stresses that aggression is frequently a sign of unmet emotional needs, overwhelming stress, or even trauma. When children lash out, they're not just trying to be difficult—they're trying to communicate something they don't have the words or emotional regulation to express. This doesn't mean we excuse the behavior, but it does mean we approach it with empathy and curiosity.

Causes and Triggers of Aggression in Students

Understanding what causes or triggers aggression in students can help us prevent these outbursts before they escalate. Five common causes include:

1. **Emotional Dysregulation:** For many kids, aggression is a result of emotional dysregulation. When they're feeling overwhelmed—whether by frustration, fear, sadness, or anger—they may not have the tools to manage those feelings in a productive way. Instead, they lash out. Kristin Souers and Pete Hall, authors of *Fostering Resilient Learners*, remind us that students who have experienced trauma or instability are particularly prone to this kind of dysregulation. These kids often haven't developed the coping skills they need to handle stress, so they rely on aggression as a way to express their feelings or regain control.

2. **Fear or Anxiety:** Aggression isn't always about anger—it can also be a defense mechanism triggered by fear or anxiety. Dr. Monique Couvson, author of *Pushout*, points out that when kids feel threatened—whether physically, emotionally, or socially—they may act aggressively as a way to protect themselves. This might happen if a student feels unsafe, embarrassed, or worried that they're about to fail at something important. For some students, the anticipation of failure or rejection is enough to set off aggressive behavior.

3. **Unmet Needs:** Sometimes aggression arises when students feel that their needs—whether for attention, control, or autonomy—aren't being met. If students feel powerless in the classroom, they may act out to demand control over the situation. Dr. Ross Greene emphasizes the importance of understanding these unmet needs and addressing them proactively. He encourages teachers to collaborate with students to identify the underlying issues driving their aggression and to work together on finding solutions.

4. **Sensory Overload:** Loud noises, bright lights, chaotic environments, or sudden changes in routine can trigger aggression in students who are sensitive to sensory input. These students might feel overwhelmed by stimuli that others don't even notice, leading to frustration and aggressive outbursts.

5. **Peer Conflicts:** Social dynamics can be a big trigger for aggression, especially if a student is being bullied, excluded, or involved in ongoing conflicts with their peers. In these cases, aggression may be a way for the student to defend themselves or assert dominance in a situation where they feel vulnerable.

Supportive Strategies for Addressing Aggression

So, how do we address aggression in a way that doesn't just stop the behavior but also supports students in developing healthier coping mechanisms? It's not about controlling the student—it's about understanding what they're communicating through their aggression and helping them find better ways to express themselves. You can use these six steps:

1. **Build Strong Relationships:** I know it can feel like one big eye roll to always focus on building relationships, but research does point to this being a pretty compelling factor. One of the most powerful tools for preventing and addressing aggression is a strong, positive relationship with students. When students feel connected to their teachers, they're more likely to trust them and less likely to act out. Kristin Souers and Pete Hall talk about the importance of building relationships as a foundation for behavior change. They remind us that students who feel safe, valued, and understood are more likely to respond positively to interventions.

    Start small—take time each day to check in with students, ask about their interests, and show that you care about them as a person, not just as a student. Use the 2 × 10 strategy: spend two minutes a day for 10 days having a personal conversation with the student about something non-academic. Over time, this can build trust and help students feel more secure in your classroom, reducing the likelihood of aggression.

2. **Teach Emotional Regulation:** Many students who display aggression lack the skills to regulate their emotions. Teaching these skills explicitly can make a huge difference. Dr. Lori Desautels emphasizes the need to help students recognize their emotional triggers and develop strategies for managing those emotions. This might include mindfulness exercises, breathing techniques, or grounding exercises to help students calm down when they feel themselves getting upset.

    Consider creating a "calm-down corner" in your classroom where students can go when they're feeling overwhelmed. Stock it with sensory tools like stress balls, fidgets, or calming visuals and include prompts for deep breathing or mindfulness exercises. Teach students how and when to use this space so that it becomes a proactive tool for managing emotions rather than a place to go after things have already escalated.

3. **Offer Predictability and Routine:** For students who are prone to aggression, predictability and routine are key. Dr. Marc Brackett explains that when students know what to expect and feel a sense of control over their environment, they're less likely to feel anxious or frustrated—and less likely to act out. Creating a predictable classroom routine, providing advance notice of transitions, and clearly outlining expectations can help reduce aggressive behaviors.

    Use visual schedules to show students what their day will look like and give them warnings before transitions (e.g., "In five minutes, we'll be cleaning up and moving to math"). This gives students a sense of control and helps them mentally prepare for changes, which can reduce the anxiety and frustration that often lead to aggression.

4. **Collaborate with a Multi-Disciplinary Team:** Addressing aggressive behavior effectively often requires input from a variety of professionals. *Say it with me: We are not tackling this on our own.* Collaborating with school counselors, psychologists, social workers, and administrators can provide a more comprehensive approach to supporting

the student. Dr. Monique Couvson emphasizes that a team-based approach allows for a deeper understanding of the student's needs and ensures that interventions are consistent across settings.

In some cases, developing a Behavior Intervention Plan (BIP) may be necessary. A BIP is tailored to the individual student and includes specific strategies for preventing aggressive behavior and responding effectively when it occurs. For example, the plan might include scheduled breaks for the student, a behavior chart to track progress, and rewards for positive behavior. BIPs also include plans on what to do when the target behavior occurs, which helps get all stakeholders on the same page, which is really grounding for the adults involved at the ground level.

5. **Provide Choices and Empower the Student:** Sometimes students act out because they feel powerless. Offering choices can help them regain a sense of control in a positive way. Dr. Ross Greene reminds us that when students feel like they have some autonomy, they're less likely to engage in aggressive behavior.

    Instead of telling students what to do, offer them two acceptable, controlled choices. For example, "Would you like to complete this worksheet at your desk or in the calm-down corner?" or "Would you like to work with a partner or by yourself?" Giving students options helps them feel like they have a say in what happens, which can reduce feelings of frustration and the need to assert control through aggression.

6. **Incorporate Social Emotional Learning (SEL):** Embedding SEL into your daily lessons can help all students—especially those prone to aggression—develop the emotional skills they need to succeed. SEL lessons teach students how to recognize and manage their emotions, empathize with others, and resolve conflicts in a constructive way.

    Consider starting each day with a short SEL lesson or incorporating SEL into other subject areas. You might have students role-play different conflict scenarios, practice active listening, or discuss strategies for handling frustration. The more students practice these skills, the more likely they are to use them in real life situations instead of resorting to aggression. I highly recommend learning more about social emotional learning from The Collaborative for Academic and Social Emotional Learning (CASEL), the leaders in SEL research. They have vetted SEL programs and are an excellent place to start if you plan to incorporate social emotional lessons into your schedule.

Common Challenges in Addressing Aggression

Even with the best strategies in place, addressing aggression in the classroom isn't easy. It takes time, patience, and a lot of emotional energy. Here are four of the most common challenges teachers face:

1. **It Feels Personal:** When a student is aggressive—especially if that aggression is directed at you—it can feel personal. It's hard not to take it to heart when a student yells at you or tears down your bulletin board. Dr. Lori Desautels reminds us that aggression is rarely about the teacher—it's about the student's internal struggles. Try to stay calm and remember that the students' behavior is a reflection of their emotional state, not a reflection of you.

2. **Inconsistent Support:** In some cases, students who display aggression may not receive consistent support outside of school. If the students' home environment is chaotic or if they're dealing with trauma, it can be difficult to change behavior in the classroom alone. This is why collaboration with a multi-disciplinary team is so important—students need support across multiple environments for behavior change to stick.

3. **Burnout:** Managing aggression day in and day out can be emotionally exhausting. It's important to prioritize self-care and seek support from colleagues when needed. If you're feeling burned out, talk

to a school counselor or administrator about finding ways to share the load or adjust your strategies.

4. **Stigma and Social Isolation:** Students who are frequently aggressive can become isolated from their peers, which only exacerbates the problem. Addressing aggression requires not only helping the student manage their behavior but also fostering an inclusive classroom environment where they feel accepted. This might mean facilitating conversations about empathy, using restorative practices, or setting up group activities that help the student connect with their peers.

Conclusion

Aggression in the classroom is one of the most challenging behaviors to manage, but with the right strategies and mindset, it's possible to support students in overcoming it. By building strong relationships, teaching emotional regulation, offering choices, and providing consistency, teachers can help students develop healthier ways of coping with their emotions. It's a process that requires time, patience, and empathy—but it's also an opportunity to make a profound difference in a child's life.

When we begin approaching aggression not as a problem to be fixed but as a message to be understood, we create a space where students can feel safe enough to let down their guard, learn new skills, and engage fully in the classroom. And that's what teaching is all about.

Case Study #1

Emma is a bright and curious eight-year-old girl in the 3rd grade at Maplewood Elementary School. Despite her academic abilities and clear potential, Emma has exhibited significant aggression in the classroom, making it challenging for her to engage fully in her learning and maintain positive relationships with her peers. The issue that has become a significant barrier for Emma and her teachers is her inability to manage frustration. Even the seemingly smallest setbacks—whether a mistake on a math problem, not being chosen for a group activity, or confusion over an assignment—trigger an intense reaction from her.

When Emma becomes frustrated, she frequently resorts to verbal and physical aggression. She may start by yelling or crying, and then escalate to tipping over desks, throwing chairs, or flinging classroom materials across the room. While she has never physically harmed another student or staff member, her aggressive outbursts create a sense of fear and unease in the classroom, disrupting the learning environment for everyone.

Her general education teacher, Ms. Turner, observed that Emma's frustration triggers seemed unpredictable at first though they were often tied to moments when Emma perceived herself as failing or not understanding something quickly enough. It became clear that Emma's frustration tolerance was very low and that she struggled with the emotional regulation necessary to manage that frustration.

Problem-Solving Approach

Ms. Turner realized that Emma's aggressive behavior was more than just a classroom management issue—it was a deeper emotional struggle that needed targeted support. Emma's aggression wasn't an attempt to be defiant; it was her way of communicating that she felt overwhelmed and out of control. After several episodes of aggression, Ms. Turner reached out to the school counselor, Ms. Lee, and the behavior interventionist, Mr. Jacobs, to discuss potential solutions.

The team agreed that Emma's aggressive outbursts were not sustainable for the classroom environment and that, without intervention, both Emma and her classmates would continue to be impacted. They understood that Emma needed help developing coping skills for managing frustration, but they also knew they needed to be proactive in preventing aggressive episodes before they occurred.

Team Collaboration

A team meeting was scheduled to bring together everyone who interacted with Emma regularly, including her general education teacher (Ms. Turner), the school counselor (Ms. Lee), the behavior interventionist (Mr. Jacobs), the special education teacher (Ms. Grant), and Emma's parents. The goal of the meeting was to develop a comprehensive plan to address Emma's aggression in a way that was supportive and constructive.

Ms. Turner began by sharing her observations about Emma's triggers, including her tendency to become aggressive when faced with challenges that she perceived as failures. Emma's parents echoed these concerns, explaining that Emma had always struggled with frustration at home as well, particularly when tasks became difficult or when she felt like she was not meeting expectations.

Ms. Lee, the school counselor, emphasized the importance of building Emma's emotional regulation skills. She explained that Emma's aggression was likely a result of feeling emotionally overwhelmed and not having the tools to manage those big feelings in the moment. Mr. Jacobs, the behavior interventionist, added that they needed to focus on preventing Emma's outbursts by identifying her triggers and developing proactive strategies to help her feel in control before her frustration escalated to aggression.

Together, the team agreed that they would design an intervention plan that included both proactive measures and reactive strategies to support Emma in managing her frustration and preventing aggressive behavior.

Designing the Intervention

The intervention plan was designed with two main components: teaching Emma replacement behaviors for managing frustration and implementing proactive strategies to prevent her from reaching a point of aggression. The team wanted to ensure that Emma had the tools to recognize when she was becoming frustrated and the strategies to de-escalate big emotions before the aggression took over. They decided on five steps:

1. **Replacement Behavior for Aggression:** The team decided to teach Emma specific emotional regulation skills that she could use when she started feeling frustrated. This included teaching her to recognize the early signs of frustration (tight chest, clenched fists, racing thoughts) and to use coping strategies like deep breathing, counting to 10, or asking for a break.

2. **Calm-Down Corner:** Ms. Turner and Mr. Jacobs set up a "calm-down corner" in the classroom where students could go if they started feeling overwhelmed. The corner was equipped with sensory tools (such as stress balls and fidget toys), calming visuals (like pictures of nature and soft colors), and a few prompts to remind students of their coping strategies. Emma was also provided with a "break card" that she could use to signal that she needed a few minutes in the calm-down corner without having to verbalize it.

3. **Social Emotional Learning (SEL) Lessons:** Ms. Lee recommended that the entire class participate in explicit SEL lessons to build empathy and emotional regulation skills. The goal was to create a supportive classroom environment where students understood emotions and had tools to manage their own. This approach would also reduce the stigma Emma might feel about using the calm-down corner.

4. **Visual and Verbal Cues:** The team agreed to implement visual and verbal cues to help Emma recognize when she was becoming frustrated. Ms. Turner would use a "traffic light" system, where a green card meant Emma was calm and focused, a yellow card indicated that she was becoming frustrated, and a red card signaled that she needed to use a coping strategy immediately. This system would provide Emma with external feedback about her emotional state. Ms. Turner kept the visuals small and on her lanyard to make them

more discrete but still visually supportive to Emma during stressful moments.

5. **Clearing the Classroom:** The team recognized that even with supports in place, Emma would likely experience aggressive moments at times. Ms. Turner shared that the class was so disrupted when Emma had aggressive episodes, and that she'd like to try radioing for assistance in her classroom and then removing the rest of the students from the class. The team worked with the administrative assistant and principal to determine that the multipurpose room could be a calm spot in the school where the class could move to during these moments. The hope was that the class could continue learning and that the behavioral support person would not have to move Emma from the classroom while she is in an aggressive state.

Implementing the Intervention

With the intervention plan in place, the team began implementing it in the classroom. Ms. Turner introduced the calm-down corner to the entire class as a space anyone could use when they were feeling overwhelmed. She explained that the calm-down corner wasn't a punishment, but a tool to help students feel better and get back to learning when they were struggling with big emotions.

Emma was introduced to her specific tools during individual sessions with Mr. Jacobs, who worked with her to practice recognizing her frustration triggers and using the calm-down corner before her frustration escalated into aggression. They also practiced using her break card and deep breathing exercises during non-stressful times so that Emma would feel comfortable using them when she needed them.

Personalized Support

In addition to the classroom-based strategies, Emma received personalized support from Ms. Lee, the school counselor. They met weekly to talk about Emma's emotions, frustrations and how she could better manage them. Ms. Lee worked with Emma on identifying her triggers and practicing different ways to respond to them. They also role-played scenarios where Emma might become frustrated and practiced using her new coping strategies in a safe and supportive environment.

Educating the Class

To foster a more supportive environment for Emma and her classmates, Ms. Turner began incorporating SEL lessons into the daily routine. These lessons focused on recognizing and managing emotions, practicing empathy, and using conflict resolution strategies. The goal was to build a classroom culture where students were more aware of their own emotions and better equipped to support one another.

The class also participated in a lesson on the brain and emotions, where they learned about the "upstairs brain" (the thinking brain) and the "downstairs brain" (the emotional brain). This lesson, based on Dr. Dan Siegel's work, helped students understand why they might feel overwhelmed at times and what they could do to regain control. Emma's classmates were encouraged to use these strategies themselves, creating a classroom environment where emotional regulation was a shared goal.

Monitoring Progress

The team monitored Emma's progress closely by tracking the frequency and intensity of her aggressive outbursts, her use of the calm-down corner, and her ability to engage with her coping strategies. Ms. Turner kept a daily log of Emma's behavior, noting both positive developments and areas where Emma was still struggling.

Mr. Jacobs met with Emma regularly to review her progress and adjust the strategies as needed. Ms. Lee continued her weekly check-ins with Emma to ensure she was feeling supported and to work through any new challenges that arose.

Initial Challenges

As expected, the intervention did not lead to immediate results. In the first few weeks, Emma struggled to use her coping strategies consistently. She often became frustrated so quickly that she forgot about the calm-down corner or her break card. There were still moments when Emma tipped over desks or threw objects before she could regain control. During these moments, the class would evacuate the room and continue learning in the multipurpose room, while Mr. Jacobs supported Emma's de-escalation in the classroom.

Emma was also hesitant to use the calm-down corner in front of her peers, fearing that they would see her as different or weak. This reluctance led to a few moments where she tried to "power through" her frustration, only for it to escalate into aggression when she could no longer manage her emotions.

Positive Developments

Despite the initial challenges, there were also many positive signs of progress. After several weeks, Emma began using the calm-down corner more regularly, and her outbursts became less frequent and aggressive. She started to recognize her frustration triggers earlier and was able to use her break card to take a moment before her frustration escalated into aggression.

Emma also began participating more in the SEL lessons, asking questions about emotions and offering examples from her own experiences. Her classmates, too, became more supportive, often reminding her to use her coping strategies when they noticed she was becoming frustrated.

Adjustments and Future Steps

Recognizing that Emma was making progress but still needed more support, the team made several adjustments to the intervention. They decided to create a more structured schedule for Emma, incorporating regular check-ins with Ms. Turner throughout the day to assess how she was feeling and provide reminders to use her strategies.

Ms. Lee also introduced a visual schedule for Emma that included "break times" throughout the day where Emma could go to the calm-down corner or take a short walk around the hallway to reset.

Continuous Support

The team agreed that continuous support would be essential for Emma's long-term success. Regular meetings with the school counselor, ongoing check-ins with her teachers, and continued reinforcement of her coping strategies would be necessary to ensure that Emma didn't revert back to her aggressive behaviors.

They also planned to meet with Emma's parents regularly to discuss her progress and ensure that the strategies used in the classroom could be reinforced at home.

Conclusion

Emma's journey toward managing her frustration and reducing her aggression in the classroom was a challenging one, but the team's collaborative approach made a significant difference. By focusing on teaching her replacement behaviors, providing her with proactive strategies, and fostering a supportive classroom environment, Emma was able to make meaningful progress.

While Emma's aggression didn't disappear overnight, the team's persistence, empathy, and commitment to her emotional well-being helped her develop healthier ways of coping with frustration. As Emma continues to grow and develop, her teachers and support staff will be there to help her build on these skills and navigate the challenges ahead.

Case Study #2

Elijah is a 10-year-old, 5th-grade student at Franklin Elementary School. Elijah loves sports, especially basketball and football, and has three younger sisters who also attend Franklin Elementary School. Elijah has recently become an avid reader and has shown a big interest in graphic novels. Elijah also started exhibiting significant aggression, particularly when he feels threatened or perceives an injustice. His aggressive tendencies have manifested in physical altercations with peers, especially during unstructured times like recess or in competitive environments such as Physical Education (PE) class. These outbursts have left his teachers and peers wary and have created a cycle of conflict that makes it difficult for Elijah to focus on academics, participate in group activities, or form meaningful relationships.

The general education teacher, Mr. Bryant, noticed that Elijah's aggressive behavior often escalates quickly, seemingly without warning. For example, during a simple classroom game or activity, Elijah can appear calm one moment but become defensive or agitated the next if he perceives that something unfair has occurred. Similarly, in PE class, if Elijah feels that he has been cheated during a game or that a peer has not followed the rules, he will often escalate from verbal confrontations to physical aggression within seconds.

Elijah also seems to be hypervigilant, constantly on edge and scanning his environment for potential threats. His peers have described him as "jumpy," and he frequently reacts with intense emotions to relatively minor incidents, such as accidentally being bumped in the hallway or overhearing an offhand comment that he interprets as criticism. Mr. Bryant has observed that Elijah can "go from zero to sixty" in terms of his emotional response, turning small events into major incidents that disrupt the classroom environment and leave Elijah feeling isolated and defensive.

Problem-Solving Approach

Recognizing that Elijah's aggression was creating a barrier to his success in school, Mr. Bryant and the school's administration initially implemented a series of disciplinary measures aimed at curbing his behavior. These measures included sending Elijah to the principal's office after incidents, suspending him for a day following physical fights, and removing him from PE class temporarily. Unfortunately, while these punitive measures provided short-term relief for the immediate problem, they did not lead to long-term behavioral improvements.

It became clear to Mr. Bryant and the school staff that punishment alone was not an effective strategy. Elijah's aggression persisted, and he began to express feelings of frustration, shame, and confusion about why he was always in trouble. He seemed to have difficulty understanding why his aggressive responses were inappropriate, especially in situations where he felt justified in defending himself or standing up for what he perceived to be an injustice.

In light of this, Mr. Bryant realized that the team needed to take a different approach. The goal would no longer be just to stop Elijah's aggressive behavior, but to address the root causes of his aggression, teach him emotional regulation skills, and provide him with alternative strategies for handling conflict.

Team Collaboration

A multidisciplinary team was formed to address Elijah's aggressive behavior and create a more comprehensive intervention plan. This team included Mr. Bryant (general education teacher), Mrs. Wilson (the school counselor), Mr. James (the PE teacher), Ms. Torres (the special education teacher), and Mrs. Harris (the school principal). Elijah's parents were also brought into the conversation to provide input and collaborate on strategies that could be reinforced both at home and at school.

During the initial team meeting, all members shared their observations about Elijah's behavior and discussed potential triggers for his aggression. Mr. Bryant emphasized the importance of understanding Elijah's hypervigilance and how small triggers, such as a perceived injustice or unexpected physical contact, could escalate quickly. Mrs. Wilson, the school counselor, noted that Elijah's hypervigilance and defensiveness could be related to underlying anxiety or past trauma and suggested that the team consider these factors when designing the intervention.

Elijah's parents confirmed that he had always been sensitive to perceived unfairness and that he often became angry and defensive when he felt that others were not following the rules. They also mentioned that Elijah had been involved in a few minor physical altercations in the past, both at school and in the neighborhood, when he felt that other children were being unfair or disrespectful toward him. Elijah was also removed from a community basketball team because he engaged in a physical fight with another athlete. This was a big source of shame for Elijah, and his parents shared that he never wanted to talk about it.

Together, the team agreed that Elijah needed support in learning how to manage his emotions, particularly in high-stress situations like recess, PE class, and other unstructured or competitive environments. They also agreed that punitive measures were not sufficient and that the focus needed to shift toward teaching Elijah alternative ways to handle his frustration and aggression.

Designing the Intervention

The team set out to design an intervention plan that would address Elijah's specific needs and provide him with the tools to manage his emotions more effectively. The intervention plan focused on three key components: emotional regulation, conflict resolution, and proactive support during high-risk situations.

1. **Emotional Regulation:** The team agreed that Elijah needed to learn how to recognize his emotions before they escalated into aggression. Mrs. Wilson, the school counselor, would work with Elijah on emotional regulation techniques, such as deep breathing exercises, mindfulness practices, and progressive muscle relaxation. Elijah would also learn to identify the early warning signs of frustration and anger, such as a racing heart, clenched fists, or shallow breathing, so that he could intervene before his emotions escalated out of control.

2. **Conflict Resolution and Replacement Behaviors:** Mr. Bryant and Ms. Torres, the special education teacher, would work with Elijah to develop specific conflict resolution skills. This included teaching him how to communicate his feelings assertively rather than aggressively, how to walk away from situations that were becoming heated, and how to seek help from an adult when needed. The team also worked on identifying replacement behaviors for physical aggression, such as using his words to express frustration or taking a break to calm down. These words and statements would be explicitly taught and practiced during sessions.

3. **Proactive Support During High-Risk Situations:** The team recognized that Elijah needed extra support during times when he was most likely to become aggressive, such as recess and PE class. Mr. James, the PE teacher, agreed to provide more structured activities during PE that emphasized teamwork and cooperation rather than competition. Additionally, a "safe zone" would be established on the playground where Elijah could go if he started to feel overwhelmed. A designated staff member would check in with Elijah periodically during these high-risk times to provide support and prevent conflicts from escalating.

Components of the Intervention

The intervention plan included five key components designed to address Elijah's aggression and help him develop healthier coping mechanisms:

1. **Morning Check-Ins:** Every morning, Elijah would check in with Mrs. Wilson before joining his class. This check-in would give Elijah an opportunity to express any concerns or anxieties he was feeling and to mentally prepare for the day ahead. Mrs. Wilson would also remind Elijah of the emotional regulation strategies they had been practicing and encourage him to use them throughout the day.

2. **Visual Reminders and Cues:** Elijah was provided with visual reminders of his emotional regulation strategies, such as a laminated card that he could keep in his desk with pictures of deep breathing exercises, a stop sign to remind him to pause before reacting, and a list of calming techniques. These visual cues would serve as reminders to Elijah during moments of frustration.

3. **Peer Mediation and Problem-Solving:** To help Elijah improve his conflict resolution skills, Mrs. Wilson would conduct peer mediation sessions with Elijah and any students involved in conflicts. These sessions would allow Elijah to practice expressing his feelings in a calm and respectful manner, while also listening to the perspectives of his peers. The goal was to teach Elijah how to resolve conflicts without resorting to aggression.

4. **Structured Recess and PE Activities:** Mr. James restructured his PE lessons for six weeks to focus on non-competitive games and cooperative activities. These changes were intended to reduce the likelihood of Elijah becoming triggered by competition. After six weeks, more competitive games and traditional PE activities would be phased in. Additionally, recess supervisors were instructed to closely monitor Elijah during free play and to intervene early if they noticed any signs of conflict.

5. **Safe Space for Breaks:** Elijah was given access to a designated "safe space" in the school building where he could go if he started feeling overwhelmed or agitated. This space, located near the counselor's office, was equipped with sensory tools, calming visuals, and a journal where Elijah could write down his thoughts and feelings.

Implementing the Intervention

The intervention was gradually implemented over the course of several weeks, starting with Elijah's morning check-ins with Mrs. Wilson. Initially, Elijah was hesitant to participate in the emotional regulation exercises and peer mediation sessions, expressing frustration that he was being singled out. However, with consistent support and encouragement from the team, Elijah began to engage more actively in the process.

Mr. Bryant and Ms. Torres worked closely with Elijah during class to help him use his visual cues and reminders. When Elijah became frustrated during academic tasks, they would remind him to take deep breaths and to use his stop sign card to pause before reacting. Over time, Elijah became more comfortable using these tools, and the frequency of his outbursts in the classroom began to decrease.

At recess and PE, the structured activities and additional supervision helped to reduce the number of conflicts Elijah was involved in. When conflicts did arise, the staff was able to intervene earlier, preventing them from escalating into physical altercations. Elijah also began to use the safe space more frequently when he felt overwhelmed, taking breaks to calm down before returning to the classroom.

Personalized Support

To further support Elijah, the team developed a personalized plan for addressing his specific triggers. This plan included working with Elijah on identifying the types of situations that were most likely to trigger his aggression, such as feeling cheated during a game or being teased by a peer. Elijah was encouraged to reflect on these triggers during his check-ins with Mrs. Wilson, and they worked together to develop personalized strategies for managing these situations.

Ms. Torres also provided Elijah with academic support, helping him break down challenging tasks into smaller, more manageable steps. This reduced Elijah's frustration during difficult assignments and gave him more opportunities to experience success.

Educating the Class

Recognizing that Elijah's aggressive behavior had affected his relationships with his peers, Mr. Bryant implemented a series of classwide lessons on empathy, emotional regulation, and conflict resolution. These lessons were designed to help all students develop a better understanding of their own emotions and the emotions of others and to create a more supportive classroom environment.

The class also participated in a restorative circle after one of Elijah's physical altercations, where students had the opportunity to express their feelings and talk about how the incident had impacted them. Elijah was given a chance to apologize to his classmates and explain what he was working on in terms of managing his emotions. This restorative practice helped to repair some of the relationships that had been damaged by Elijah's aggression and fostered a greater sense of community within the class.

Monitoring Progress

The team closely monitored Elijah's progress by tracking the frequency and intensity of his aggressive moments, his use of the safe space, and his participation in the peer mediation sessions. Weekly meetings were held to discuss Elijah's progress and to make any necessary adjustments to the intervention plan.

Initial Challenges

While the intervention led to some early successes, there were still challenges along the way. Elijah sometimes struggled to use his emotional regulation strategies consistently, especially in high-stress situations. There were moments when Elijah reverted to his old patterns of aggression, particularly when he felt that he had been wronged by a peer. The team recognized that changing deeply ingrained behaviors would take time and continued to provide Elijah with support and encouragement.

Positive Developments

As the weeks went on, Elijah began to show more progress. He started to use his safe space more proactively, often removing himself from situations before they escalated into conflicts. His aggressive incidents became less frequent, and when conflicts did arise, Elijah was more likely to seek help from an adult rather than resort to aggression.

Elijah's relationships with his peers also began to improve. The peer mediation sessions helped Elijah build better communication skills, and his classmates started to see him in a more positive light. Elijah's participation in group activities increased, and he began to enjoy cooperative games in PE without becoming overly competitive or defensive.

Adjustments and Future Steps

Based on Elijah's progress, the team made several adjustments to the intervention plan. They decided to gradually reduce the frequency of his morning check-ins with Mrs. Wilson, allowing Elijah to take more ownership of his emotional regulation strategies. However, they agreed to keep the safe space available to Elijah for as long as he needed it.

The team also discussed the possibility of involving Elijah in a peer leadership program, where he could use his growing conflict resolution skills to help mediate disputes between other students. This would give Elijah an opportunity to practice his skills in a positive and constructive way.

Continuous Support

While Elijah had made significant progress, the team recognized that he would need ongoing support to maintain his gains and continue developing his emotional regulation skills. Regular check-ins with the counselor, continued use of the safe space, and periodic peer mediation sessions would remain part of his support plan. The team also planned to meet with Elijah's parents regularly to ensure that the strategies used at school could be reinforced at home.

Conclusion

Elijah's story highlights the complexity of managing aggression in the classroom, particularly when that aggression is rooted in hypervigilance and emotional dysregulation. By shifting the focus from punitive measures to proactive support and skill-building, the team was able to help Elijah develop healthier ways of managing his emotions and handling conflict. No longer were band-aid measures the norm, but actual behavior change and support became the focus. This is a true example of a student centered intervention.

Through collaboration, empathy, and patience, the team helped Elijah reduce his aggressive behavior, improve his relationships with his peers, and engage more fully in the learning environment. While the journey was not without its challenges, the progress Elijah made demonstrates the power of a comprehensive, individualized approach to addressing aggressive behavior in the classroom.

CHAPTER EIGHT

Inattention

WE ALL encounter a wide range of learning styles and behaviors in our classrooms, and one of the trickiest yet most common behaviors we see is inattention and hyperactivity. For many students, these behaviors are symptomatic of conditions like ADHD, anxiety, trauma, or sensory processing difficulties. Regardless of the root cause, inattention and hyperactivity present significant barriers to learning and engagement. It's important to remember that it's not our job to diagnose kids and give them labels, we can only help accommodate the kids in front of us to help them reach their greatest potential. Addressing these behaviors requires a compassionate, informed approach, focusing on evidence-based interventions that support students' unique needs.

Recognizing Inattention as a Barrier to Learning and Engagement

Inattention often manifests in subtle ways that can be easily overlooked or misinterpreted as defiance or laziness. But in reality, inattention can be a significant barrier to a student's ability to engage meaningfully with the curriculum. This lack of focus can result in missed instructions, incomplete assignments, and difficulty maintaining relationships with peers. Students who are inattentive may appear disconnected or overwhelmed, struggling to stay on task even when they appear to be trying.

Dr. Lori Desautels emphasizes that inattention can actually be a symptom of dysregulated nervous systems. Students who have experienced trauma, for example, may have difficulty focusing because their brain is constantly scanning for potential threats. Dr. Bruce Perry adds that for children struggling with persistent inattention, the brain is likely processing information differently, making it harder for them to filter out distractions and focus on the task at hand.

Inattention isn't just a behavior; it's a neurological response to internal or external stimuli. Recognizing this helps us reframe the issue: Students who are inattentive or hyperactive aren't choosing to disengage—they are often unable to engage due to factors beyond their control. Understanding these root causes is essential for providing the right support.

Causes and Triggers of Inattention in Students

Inattention in students can arise from a variety of causes, each requiring a different approach to support:

- **ADHD and Neurological Differences:** Students with ADHD have brains that process stimuli differently than neurotypical students. Their brains struggle with executive functioning skills—such as organization, time management, and task initiation—that are crucial for academic success. These students may appear restless or unable to focus for extended periods, not because they lack discipline but because their brains are wired differently. Again, even if we suspect a child has ADHD, it's not our role as educators to make that diagnosis. We can accommodate and support the kids in front of us though!

- **Trauma and Stress:** Children who have experienced trauma may be stuck in a state of hypervigilance, always on guard for potential threats. This can make it incredibly difficult for them to focus on academic tasks, as their brain prioritizes survival over learning.

- **Sensory Processing Difficulties:** Some students are more sensitive to environmental stimuli like noise, light, or movement, which can be overwhelming and lead to inattention. In these cases, students may need specific sensory supports to help them stay calm and focused.

- **Anxiety:** Students with anxiety may struggle to focus because their minds are preoccupied with worries about the future, their social standing, or their academic performance. In some cases, their inattention may be a way to avoid confronting these fears directly.

- **Sleep Deprivation or Health Issues:** Students who aren't getting enough sleep or who have underlying health issues like allergies or undiagnosed vision problems may find it difficult to focus simply because their bodies and brains are not functioning optimally.

Recognizing these possible causes helps us approach inattention with empathy, understanding that it's not simply a matter of students choosing to tune out but rather a reflection of deeper neurological or emotional challenges.

Supportive Strategies for Addressing Inattention

Supporting students with inattention and hyperactivity requires a toolbox of strategies that can be adopted to meet the unique needs of each student. Here are some research-backed, practical interventions that can help students stay engaged in the classroom.

Explicit Teaching of Executive Functioning Skills

Executive functioning skills—like organization, time management, task initiation, and flexible thinking—are often underdeveloped in students with attention difficulties. These skills form the foundation for learning, yet many students struggle with them because they are abstract and difficult to grasp without direct instruction. As teachers, we can provide explicit teaching of these skills to help students develop more effective learning strategies.

Using social scripts or step-by-step instructions for tasks can help demystify these concepts. For example, breaking down how to start a writing assignment into smaller, manageable steps—brainstorming, organizing ideas, writing a draft—can help students initiate and complete tasks more effectively. Reinforcing these behaviors through consistent feedback can create positive habits over time.

Providing Sensory Supports

Sensory tools can be invaluable for students with attention difficulties, especially those who have trouble filtering out distractions. Simple sensory supports, like stress balls, glitter jars, or even weighted blankets, can help students self-regulate and stay focused on their work. These tools give students a way to channel their restlessness in a non-disruptive way.

For students who need more frequent sensory input, creating a sensory-friendly space within the classroom can be helpful. This might include a quiet corner with dim lighting, noise-reducing headphones, and soft textures where students can go to self-regulate before returning to their work.

Creating Visually Calm Environments

Classroom environments filled with bright colors, posters, and other busy stimuli can be overwhelming for students with attention needs or sensory sensitivities. Research has shown that visually overstimulating environments can detract from students' ability to focus. (Fisher et al., 2014) By keeping the classroom decor simple and functionally designed, teachers can create a calmer space that allows students to concentrate on their learning.

This might mean using neutral colors on the walls, minimizing clutter, and avoiding excessive decorations that can pull attention away from the tasks at hand. Visual schedules and clearly labeled areas for materials can also help students with attention difficulties stay organized and know what to expect throughout the day.

Visual Timers and Structured Breaks

Students with this profile may often struggle with open-ended tasks because they have difficulty understanding how much time they need to stay focused. Visual timers can provide a concrete way for students to see how long they need to work on a task before they get a break. For instance, setting a timer for 15 minutes of focused work followed by a 5-minute break can help students pace themselves and feel less overwhelmed.

Breaks are crucial for students who struggle with attention, especially when they involve movement. Scheduling short, frequent breaks that involve physical activity—like stretching, walking, or doing yoga—can help students release pent-up energy and refocus on their work.

Incorporating Movement into Lessons

Many students with hyperactivity benefit from opportunities to move throughout the day. Sitting still for long periods is often difficult for them, so incorporating movement into lessons can help them stay engaged. This might include having students stand up while working, using flexible seating options like yoga balls or standing desks, or incorporating kinesthetic learning activities into the lesson.

Incorporating physical movement into lessons, such as having students act out vocabulary words or solve math problems by moving around the room, can also be a way to engage their bodies while stimulating their minds.

Calm Corners and Safe Spaces

Creating a calm corner in the classroom can provide students with a designated space to go when they are feeling overwhelmed or overstimulated.

This space should be stocked with calming items, such as sensory tools, pillows, breathing exercise visuals, and simple books. Having a calm space can give students a break from the hustle and bustle of the classroom and help them self-regulate before returning to their work.

Dr. Marc Brackett emphasizes that providing students with opportunities to regulate their emotions in a safe, non-judgmental space helps them manage their attention better in the long run.

Teaching Self-Advocacy

One of the most empowering tools we can give students with attention difficulties is the ability to advocate for their own needs. Encouraging students to express when they need a break, when they feel overwhelmed, or when they need extra help helps them take control of their learning.

Students can be taught to write letters or notes to teachers and paraprofessionals explaining their learning preferences and what strategies work best for them. This not only empowers students but also gives teachers valuable insights into how to support each individual more effectively.

Positive Reinforcement and Clear Expectations

Setting clear expectations for behavior and providing positive reinforcement when students meet those expectations is essential. For students with attention difficulties, it's important to provide feedback that is specific and immediate. Instead of simply saying, "Good job," provide praise that is tied directly to the behavior you're reinforcing: "Great work staying focused on your reading for 15 minutes!"

Providing clear expectations also means outlining the steps for what happens if a student becomes distracted or off-task. Creating a system of gentle reminders, visual cues, and consistent routines helps students understand what is expected of them and gives them the structure they need to stay engaged.

Common Challenges in Addressing Inattention in the Classroom

While these strategies can be incredibly effective, they are not without challenges.

Time Constraints

Finding the time to implement individualized supports for students with attention difficulties can be difficult, especially when teachers are balancing the needs of an entire classroom. To manage this, try incorporating these strategies into whole-class routines whenever possible. For example, using visual timers and movement breaks for the entire class not only benefits students with attention needs but also helps maintain overall classroom engagement.

Inconsistent Progress

Students with attention difficulties may experience inconsistent progress. One day they might be focused and engaged, and the next, they might be entirely off-task. This inconsistency can be frustrating, but it's important to remember that attention regulation is a skill that takes time to develop. Patience, persistence, and flexibility are key.

Peer Dynamics and Stigma

Students who struggle with inattention and hyperactivity may face social challenges as well. Their behaviors may lead to misunderstandings with peers or even social isolation. It's essential to foster a classroom culture of empathy and understanding, where students recognize that everyone has different strengths and challenges.

Dr. Monique Couvson suggests using explicit social emotional learning (SEL) strategies and lessons to teach empathy and encourage positive peer interactions. Teaching all students about neurodiversity can help reduce stigma and create a more inclusive classroom environment.

Conclusion

Inattention and hyperactivity are significant challenges in the classroom, but with the right strategies, teachers can support students in developing the skills they need to succeed. By recognizing the root causes of inattention—whether they stem from ADHD, trauma, anxiety, or sensory processing difficulties—it honestly doesn't matter. Teachers can provide targeted interventions that help students engage with their learning in meaningful ways.

With the use of structured environments, sensory supports, movement breaks, and explicit instruction in executive functioning skills, teachers can help students with inattention and hyperactivity thrive.

Case Study #1

Mason is a bright and imaginative 1st grader with a passion for animals and an impressive ability to remember facts about dinosaurs. His inquisitive nature shines through in his love for asking questions, and he often surprises his teachers with his creativity and ideas when he is engaged. However, Mason's significant difficulties with inattention have created barriers to his academic success and have impacted his ability to fully engage in the classroom environment.

From the beginning of the school year, Mason's general education teacher, Ms. Turner, noticed that his ability to remain focused during lessons and transitions was extremely limited. While the class sat on the rug for circle time or story reading, Mason would roll around, fidget, and often blurt out answers or unrelated comments without raising his hand. Ms. Turner had established clear routines and expectations for her students, regularly reminding them of classroom rules like waiting for their turn to speak and sitting in their designated spots during lessons. Despite these reminders and her best efforts to reinforce positive behavior, Mason continued to struggle with self-regulation.

Additionally, when Ms. Turner gave directions for class activities or transitions, Mason frequently seemed confused or unsure about what to do next. He would often ask peers for clarification, or just find something else to do that was his own plan. His frequent off-task behavior during instructional times often resulted in him missing important information, leaving him unsure about how to proceed with assigned tasks. This inattention led to frustration for Mason and his teacher, and sometimes resulted in Mason becoming withdrawn or resistant to participate.

Problem-Solving Approach

Ms. Turner began documenting Mason's behavior to better understand when and why these challenges were occurring. She noticed that Mason's inattention was most pronounced during whole-group instruction and transitions. He struggled to stay still and focused during circle time, math, and reading lessons, often rolling around on the rug, playing with objects, or getting distracted by things around him. This behavior disrupted his own learning and that of his peers. When asked to complete independent work, Mason frequently seemed confused and unsure of what to do, which resulted in him either doing nothing, or blurting out unrelated comments in an effort to avoid his frustration.

At first, Ms. Turner used traditional disciplinary measures to address Mason's behavior. These included verbal reminders, moving his seat closer to the teacher, and occasionally sending him to a "thinking spot" in the classroom when he was particularly disruptive. While these measures sometimes helped in the short term, they did not lead to lasting changes in Mason's behavior. He would return to his seat and quickly resume his rolling, blurting, and off-task behavior. Ms. Turner realized that simply addressing the symptoms of Mason's behavior without understanding the underlying causes was not going to lead to success.

Team Collaboration

Recognizing the need for a more comprehensive approach, Ms. Turner reached out to the school's special education team for support. A meeting was convened with the school's special education teacher, Mrs. Douglas; the school counselor, Mr. Johnson; and the school psychologist, Dr. Lee. Mason's parents were also invited to the meeting to provide their input and to help create a plan that would address Mason's needs both at home and in school.

During the meeting, Mason's parents shared that they had noticed similar behaviors at home. Mason often had difficulty staying focused during family activities like reading or games, and they frequently had to give him repeated reminders to follow through with tasks like getting dressed or completing chores. Mason's parents also shared that he had always been an active child, frequently bouncing from one activity to the next. They were open to the school taking a proactive approach to support Mason and expressed a desire to stay in the loop. His parents shared that they didn't have major concerns and saw Mason's behavior as pretty typical of an average first grader.

Designing the Intervention

The team agreed that Mason's behaviors were likely related to challenges with attention regulation, self-control, and possibly sensory processing. To address these challenges, they decided to create a multi-tiered intervention plan focused on explicit teaching of self-regulation skills, providing sensory supports, and breaking tasks down into manageable steps for Mason.

1. **Behavioral Support Plan:** The team decided that Mason needed explicit instruction in self-regulation strategies. Mrs. Douglas suggested implementing a simple self-regulation chart that would allow Mason to visually monitor his own behavior throughout the day. The chart would have smiley faces for each activity (e.g., morning

meeting, math, reading) and a place for Mason to color in how he felt he performed during that activity. This would be paired with praise and positive reinforcement for staying on task.

2. **Sensory Supports:** Given Mason's fidgeting and rolling during circle time, Mr. Johnson suggested introducing sensory tools that would help Mason manage his need for movement without disrupting the class. A sensory cushion, weighted lap pad, and fidget tools would be made available to Mason during times when he needed to sit for longer periods. Additionally, the team agreed to set up a designated "calm corner" in the classroom where Mason could go if he started to feel overwhelmed or needed a sensory break.

3. **Visual and Verbal Supports:** Dr. Lee recommended that instructions be broken down into smaller, more manageable steps for Mason. She suggested using visual supports like picture schedules and visual timers to help Mason stay on track. Ms. Turner agreed to pair verbal directions with these visual cues to ensure that Mason could better understand and follow along with what was expected of him. He was given his own visual timer and would be able to decorate it with animal stickers for additional motivation and personalization. An example of a visual checklist can be accessed at the QR code below.

4. **Check-Ins and Individualized Support:** To further support Mason, it was decided that he would have daily check-ins with Mr. Johnson, the school counselor, to talk about his progress, celebrate successes, and discuss any challenges. These check-ins would also serve as an opportunity for Mason to practice self-advocacy skills and learn how to express his feelings when he was feeling frustrated or overwhelmed.

Components of the Intervention

The intervention plan for Mason included the following components:

- **Self-Regulation Chart:** Mason would use a simple smiley face chart to reflect on his behavior during different parts of the day. This chart would be used to encourage self-reflection and reinforce positive behavior through praise and rewards.
- **Sensory Supports:** Mason would have access to sensory tools, including a fidget spinner, weighted lap pad, and sensory cushion during whole-group instruction. He could also visit the calm corner if he felt overwhelmed or needed a break.
- **Visual and Verbal Supports:** Ms. Turner would use visual schedules, timers, and picture cues to break down tasks and provide additional support for Mason during transitions and independent work.
- **Check-Ins with the School Counselor:** Mason would have daily 3 minute check-ins with Mr. Johnson to discuss his behavior, feelings, and progress in managing his attention and self-regulation.

Implementing the Intervention

Once the intervention plan was finalized, Ms. Turner began implementing the various strategies in her classroom. Mason's self-regulation chart was introduced during morning circle time, and Ms. Turner spent time teaching Mason how to use it. She modeled how to reflect on his behavior and praised him when he accurately identified his efforts to stay on task. Mason was also given access to his sensory tools during circle time and other whole-group activities, which seemed to immediately help him stay seated and reduce his fidgeting.

Ms. Turner also began using visual schedules and timers to provide Mason with more structured guidance during transitions and independent work. Before each task, she would walk him through the visual steps and set a timer to help him understand how long the activity would last. This helped reduce his confusion about what to do and when, and he began to rely on the visuals for guidance instead of constantly asking his peers for help.

Personalized Support

Mason's individualized check-ins with Mr. Johnson were a critical piece of the intervention. During these meetings, Mason had the opportunity to talk about his feelings and frustrations, as well as celebrate the small victories he experienced throughout the day. Mr. Johnson also worked with Mason on self-advocacy skills, teaching him how to ask for a break when he needed one and how to express his needs to adults in the classroom.

Additionally, the school psychologist, Dr. Lee, began working with Mason on mindfulness exercises to help him calm his mind and body when he felt overwhelmed. These exercises included deep breathing, counting to 10, and using positive self-talk to manage any frustration.

Educating the Class

Ms. Turner recognized that Mason's behavior had an impact on his peers, so she made an effort to educate the entire class about the importance of understanding and supporting each other's differences. She held class discussions about how everyone learns differently and how some students might need tools like fidgets or breaks to help them focus. This fostered a more inclusive and supportive environment, and Mason's classmates became more understanding of his needs.

Monitoring Progress

The team met regularly to monitor Mason's progress and make adjustments to the intervention plan as needed. Ms. Turner kept detailed notes on Mason's behavior and shared them with the team during meetings. Over time, they noticed that Mason was making improvements in his ability to stay on task during whole-group instruction. While he still had moments of distraction, he was more consistently using his sensory tools and the calm corner to manage his energy.

Mason also began to show improvement in following directions during independent work. The visual supports and timers helped him feel more confident in completing tasks, and he became less reliant on his peers or adult intervention for guidance.

Initial Challenges

While the intervention showed positive results, there were initial challenges. Mason was resistant to using the self-regulation chart at first, often claiming he didn't need it or that it was "too hard." Ms. Turner and Mr. Johnson worked patiently with him, providing gentle encouragement and making the chart more interactive by allowing Mason to choose the colors and stickers he used to mark his progress.

There were also moments when Mason became frustrated with his sensory tools, especially when he was feeling particularly overwhelmed. He would sometimes tap the fidget spinner loudly on the floor or wall, or refuse to use the sensory cushion. The team responded by offering alternatives and reminding Mason of his choices in managing his frustration.

Positive Developments

Despite these challenges, the team saw significant positive developments in Mason's behavior and engagement. Over time, Mason became more comfortable using his self-regulation chart and started to take great pride in tracking his successes. He also began to independently request sensory breaks when he felt overwhelmed, showing growth in his self-awareness and self-advocacy skills.

Mason's peers also became more supportive of his needs. They started offering encouragement when they saw him using his tools and working hard to stay on task. This created a more positive and inclusive classroom environment, which benefited both Mason and his classmates.

Adjustments and Future Steps

As Mason continued to make progress, the team made adjustments to the intervention plan to ensure that it remained effective. For example, they added more variety to Mason's sensory tools, allowing him to choose from a wider range of options depending on his needs. They also began to gradually fade the use of the self-regulation chart, encouraging Mason to rely more on internal feelings and self awareness rather than external monitoring.

The team also worked with Mason's parents to implement similar strategies at home, ensuring that he had consistent support in managing his attention and behavior across all settings. His parents did seem to notice the difference in Mason when using the provided resources, and agreed that this could be something to try at home and possibly during extracurricular activities.

Continuous Support

The team agreed that Mason would continue to receive regular check-ins with the school counselor and ongoing support from the special education teacher to help him maintain his progress. They also scheduled follow-up meetings with Mason's parents to discuss any concerns and make sure that the strategies were working effectively both at home and at school.

Conclusion

Mason's case highlights the importance of a comprehensive, collaborative approach to addressing attention and self-regulation challenges in the classroom. Through a combination of individualized supports, sensory tools, and explicit instruction, Mason was able to make significant improvements in his ability to engage in learning and manage his behavior. While challenges remained, the team's commitment to providing consistent support and making adjustments along the way ensured that Mason could continue to thrive in the classroom environment.

This case study underscores the need for empathy, patience, and collaboration in supporting students with attention difficulties. By working together, educators, parents, and specialists can create a plan that meets the unique needs of each student, helping them overcome barriers to learning and reach their full potential.

Case Study #2

Sophie is a bright, creative, and empathetic 5th-grade student who loves to draw and has a strong imagination. Her teachers often note that she brings a positive energy to the classroom and has a natural talent for art and storytelling. Sophie also displays a strong sense of fairness, often standing up for peers who are being treated unfairly, which demonstrates her empathy and kindness. Despite these strengths, Sophie has significant challenges with inattention that have affected her academic performance, social interactions, and behavior during unstructured times, especially recess.

While Sophie's teacher, Mrs. Adams, has explicitly taught routines, rules, and expectations in the classroom, Sophie still struggles to stay focused, follow directions, and engage in structured activities. Sophie often fidgets during lessons, compensates for missed instructions by guessing what she is supposed to do. Additionally, she frequently makes impulsive decisions, especially during unstructured times like recess or free periods. Mrs. Adams, along with other school stakeholders, has worked to address Sophie's behavior with various disciplinary measures, like missed recess, but these strategies have not resulted in any long-term success.

Initial Observations

In the first months of the school year, Mrs. Adams noticed that Sophie had a lot of difficulty staying focused during lessons. While the rest of the class would sit quietly and listen, Sophie frequently fidgeted, played with her hair or pencils, and seemed distracted by objects around her. At times, she would blurt out answers before thinking through the question or make unrelated comments. When Mrs. Adams would give instructions, Sophie would appear to be listening but often miss key information, leading her to ask her peers for clarification after the fact or attempt to complete tasks incorrectly due to misunderstandings.

During recess and other unstructured times, Sophie's impulsivity became more pronounced. She often made quick, unwise decisions, such as climbing the play structures in unsafe ways, cutting in line during games, or getting involved in peer conflicts that she didn't fully understand. On one occasion, she was reprimanded for throwing a ball too hard at a peer during recess, not realizing how her actions could hurt someone. Sophie's impulsive behavior often seemed to stem from a lack of forethought or awareness of potential consequences.

Mrs. Adams and her colleagues had implemented some basic disciplinary measures, such as talking to Sophie about her choices, assigning her to sit out of recess after certain incidents, or moving her seat to the front of the classroom. While these actions sometimes led to temporary improvements, they did not bring about any lasting change in Sophie's behavior or attention.

Problem-Solving Approach

Recognizing that Sophie's behavior was not improving through conventional disciplinary measures, Mrs. Adams decided to take a problem-solving approach. She began by collecting data and keeping a record of when and where Sophie's inattentive or impulsive behavior was occurring most frequently. This included tracking patterns during different parts of the day (e.g., morning vs. afternoon), as well as identifying specific situations that triggered Sophie's impulsive decision-making.

Mrs. Adams noted that Sophie's inattention was most noticeable during lengthy, teacher-led instruction and transitions between activities. Sophie struggled to sit still and follow directions when there was minimal movement or engagement in lessons. Additionally, during recess, Sophie seemed to become overwhelmed by the unstructured environment and would often act without thinking.

Team Collaboration

To address Sophie's behavior more effectively, Mrs. Adams collaborated with her co-teacher, who is the grade's special education teacher, Ms. Shah. Together they connected with Mr. Carter, the school counselor; and Dr. Wallace, the school psychologist. A meeting was scheduled with this team, as well as Sophie's parents, to discuss the challenges she was facing and brainstorm strategies for improvement.

During the meeting, Mrs. Adams shared her observations of Sophie's behavior, noting her strengths as well as her difficulties with inattention and impulsivity. Sophie's parents were supportive and eager to help, sharing that they had noticed similar behaviors at home. Sophie would often forget tasks after being given instructions, lose focus during family activities, and make impulsive decisions when playing with friends or siblings. Sophie's parents expressed concern about how these behaviors were impacting her social life and academics, but they were unsure of how to help her manage them.

Dr. Wallace suggested that Sophie's behaviors could be related to challenges with executive functioning, particularly in areas such as impulse control, working memory, and planning. Mr. Carter mentioned that Sophie might benefit from strategies that explicitly teach her how to slow down her decision-making process and think through the consequences of her actions. The team agreed that a multi-faceted intervention plan was needed to address Sophie's inattention and impulsive behavior, both in the classroom and during unstructured times.

Designing the Intervention

The team developed an intervention plan that focused on helping Sophie improve her attention, impulse control, and decision-making skills. The intervention plan included the following components:

1. **Behavioral Support Plan:** Sophie would be taught explicit strategies for improving her focus during class, such as using self-monitoring techniques and visual reminders. She would also be taught how to recognize when she was about to make an impulsive decision and use a "stop and think" strategy to pause and consider her options before acting.

2. **Sensory Supports:** Since Sophie frequently fidgeted during lessons, the team agreed to provide her with sensory tools that would allow her to move and fidget in a non-disruptive way. These tools included a fidget cube, a stress ball, and a wiggle cushion for her chair. Sophie could use these tools to help manage her energy and focus during class.

3. **Structured Recess Activities:** To help Sophie manage her impulsivity during recess, the team decided to introduce structured activities that would provide her with clear guidelines and expectations. Ms. Shah would oversee these activities, as she was regularly outside supporting other students during recess. These activities included group games, simple sports, and cooperative play with peers. These structured activities were designed to give Sophie a more predictable and controlled environment, reducing the likelihood of impulsive decisions.

4. **Social Skills Training:** Mr. Carter would work with Sophie in an already established counseling small group that focused on social skills, impulse control, and emotional regulation. These sessions would teach Sophie how to recognize and manage her emotions in social situations, as well as how to make better choices when interacting with peers.

5. **Visual Schedules and Timers:** In the classroom, Mrs. Adams and Ms. Shah would use visual schedules and timers to help Sophie stay on task and transition more smoothly between activities. These tools would provide Sophie with concrete reminders of what she needed to do and how much time she had to complete each task.

6. **Positive Reinforcement:** The team agreed to use positive reinforcement to encourage Sophie when she demonstrated improvement in her attention and decision-making. This reinforcement could include verbal praise and or being given a special responsibility in the classroom (e.g., line leader or helping with classroom pet care tasks).

Implementing the Intervention

With the intervention plan in place, Mrs. Adams began implementing the strategies in her classroom. She worked alongside Ms. Shah to introduce Sophie to the visual schedules and timers, explaining how they would help her stay focused and know what to expect throughout the day. Mrs. Adams also modeled the "stop and think" strategy for Sophie, teaching her how to pause before acting impulsively and consider the possible consequences of her choices.

Sophie was given access to her sensory tools during class, which helped reduce her fidgeting and allowed her to focus more effectively during lessons. When Sophie began to feel restless, Mrs. Adams encouraged her to use the wiggle cushion or stress ball as a way to manage her energy.

During recess, Ms. Shah began leading structured activities with Sophie and a small group of students. These activities provided Sophie with more guidance and structure, reducing the likelihood of impulsive behavior. Sophie also attended social skills training sessions with Mr. Carter, where she learned strategies for managing frustration, recognizing her emotions, and interacting more positively with her peers.

Personalized Support

The intervention plan was personalized to meet Sophie's specific needs, providing her with tools and strategies to help her focus, manage her impulses, and make better decisions. Sophie responded well to the sensory supports in the classroom, and she began to show improvement in her ability to stay seated and really attend during lessons. She also started using the "stop and think" strategy more consistently, pausing to consider her choices before acting impulsively.

The structured recess activities were particularly helpful for Sophie, as they gave her a clear framework for interacting with peers and participating in games. Sophie's behavior during recess improved significantly, with fewer instances of impulsive decisions leading to conflicts or unsafe behavior.

Educating the Class

Mrs. Adams and Ms. Shah recognized the importance of fostering a classroom culture of understanding and support for all students, including Sophie. They held class discussions about how everyone learns differently and may need different tools or strategies to help them succeed. These discussions helped to create a more inclusive environment, where students were more understanding of each other's challenges and supportive of their classmates.

Monitoring Progress

The team met regularly to monitor Sophie's progress and make adjustments to the intervention plan as needed. Mrs. Adams kept detailed notes on Sophie's behavior in the classroom, tracking her use of the sensory tools, her ability to stay focused during lessons, and her use of the "stop and think" strategy. Mr. Carter & Ms. Shah provided updates on Sophie's behavior during recess and her progress in social skills training.

Overall, the team saw positive improvements in Sophie's behavior. She was more engaged in class, better able to follow instructions, and more thoughtful in her decision-making during recess. Sophie's impulsivity decreased, and she began to develop stronger relationships with her peers as a result of her improved social interactions.

Initial Challenges

Despite the positive developments, there were initial challenges in implementing the intervention. Sophie was very uninterested in using the visual schedules and timers at first, often claiming that she didn't need them. Mrs. Adams responded by providing gentle reminders and making the schedules more interactive, allowing Sophie to mark off tasks as she completed them.

Sophie also struggled with the social skills training sessions initially, finding it difficult to apply the strategies she was learning in real-life situations. Mr. Carter provided additional support and reinforcement during recess, helping Sophie practice her new skills in a more structured environment.

Positive Developments

As the intervention progressed, Sophie became more comfortable with the strategies and began to take ownership of her behavior. She started using the visual schedules and timers more consistently, and her ability to stay on task improved. Sophie also began to apply the "stop and think" strategy more independently, pausing before acting impulsively and considering the potential outcomes of her choices.

Sophie's behavior during recess improved significantly, with fewer instances of conflicts or impulsive actions. She became more engaged in group activities and started to build stronger friendships with her peers. Sophie's confidence grew as she experienced more success in both academic and social settings.

Adjustments and Future Steps

As Sophie continued to make progress, the team made adjustments to the intervention plan to ensure that it remained effective. For example, they gradually reduced the use of the visual schedules and timers as Sophie became more independent in managing her time and attention. The team also increased the complexity of the social skills training sessions, focusing on more advanced strategies for conflict resolution and emotional regulation.

The team agreed to continue providing regular check-ins with Sophie to monitor her progress and make any necessary adjustments to the intervention plan. Sophie's parents were also involved in the process, receiving updates on her progress and implementing similar strategies at home to support her development.

Continuous Supports

The team recognized that Sophie would continue to need ongoing support to maintain her progress and develop new skills. They scheduled follow-up meetings with Sophie's parents to discuss her progress and ensure that the strategies were working effectively both at home and at school.

Conclusion

Sophie's story confirms the importance of a comprehensive, collaborative approach to addressing attention and impulse control challenges in the classroom. Through a combination of individualized supports, structured activities, and explicit instruction, Sophie was able to make significant improvements in her behavior and engagement. While challenges remained, the team's commitment to providing consistent support and making adjustments along the way ensured that Sophie could continue to thrive in the classroom environment.

CHAPTER NINE

Dishonesty

AH, THE age-old issue of lying in the classroom. Truth be told, but when I was a new teacher, I thought that catching students in a lie would be a rare occurrence. To no shock, I was wrong! It turns out that dishonesty in kids is much more common than we may think, and it's not always as straightforward as a student trying to pull a fast one over on us. When kids lie, it can be frustrating, even infuriating. It can make us question whether our students respect us, or if we're getting through to them at all. But it's important to take a step back, breathe, and recognize that dishonesty is often a symptom of something deeper going on under the surface.

Before we jump to conclusions, we need to recognize that lying is a barrier to learning and engagement. Just like any other challenging behavior, it has its causes, triggers, and solutions. If we approach dishonesty with empathy, understanding, and a few strategies up our sleeves, we'll be much more successful in helping students overcome this issue.

Recognizing Dishonesty as a Barrier to Learning and Engagement

Dishonesty in the classroom, whether it's about why homework wasn't done, an excuse for a conflict at recess, or even cheating on a test, disrupts the learning environment. When students lie, they're not just breaking trust, they're often distancing themselves from the opportunity to learn from their mistakes. It becomes a barrier to authentic engagement in their own growth and development.

As we have heard in previous chapters, Dr. Lori Desautels reminds us that all behavior, even dishonesty, is communication. Kids lie for a reason. It might be a defense mechanism, an attempt to avoid consequences, or a way to protect themselves from embarrassment. Whatever the reason, the key is to recognize that lying is a symptom of a deeper issue, not the problem itself.

We have to remember that when students lie, they're trying to tell us something. Maybe it's fear of failure, maybe it's a lack of confidence, or maybe it's something happening at home that's spilling over into the classroom. Dr. Bruce Perry emphasizes that children who have experienced trauma may use lying as a protective mechanism. It's their way of controlling a situation when they feel vulnerable or powerless. This means that instead of focusing solely on the lie, we should be asking, "What's going on here? What does this child need?"

Causes and Triggers of Dishonesty in Students

So why do kids lie? Well, there's no one-size-fits-all answer, but here are a few common causes and triggers:

1. **Fear of Consequences:** This is probably the most obvious one. If a child thinks they're going to get in trouble, lying might seem like the quickest way to avoid punishment. They might think, "If I admit to this, I'm toast," so instead, they say something that seems like a safer option, even if it's not true. There also may be some fear of notifying their guardians at home, which is another layer of a fear of consequences.

2. **Perfectionism:** Students who are perfectionists or who feel immense pressure to succeed might lie to cover up mistakes or avoid admitting they need help. Dr. Marc Brackett highlights that students often hide their true feelings behind dishonesty, especially if they're anxious or scared of disappointing others.

3. **Low Self-Esteem:** When students don't feel good about themselves, they might lie to make themselves appear more capable or more likable than they believe they are. This can manifest in students who lie about their abilities, saying they understand something when they don't, or making excuses for not completing work when the real issue is that they're struggling. We've all had the student that tells their classmates that their dad drives a race car, they have an eagle as a pet, or that they have an indoor swimming pool at their house. Creating a new, often better or more exciting, reality often seems like a probable solution to not feeling up to par.

4. **Avoidance of Responsibility:** Sometimes, lying is a way for students to avoid taking responsibility for their actions. If a student didn't study for a test, they might claim they lost the study guide rather than admit they didn't put in the effort.

5. **Desire for Attention:** Lying can also be a way for students to get attention. This might happen with students who feel overlooked or who aren't getting their needs met in other ways. They might exaggerate stories or tell lies about others to insert themselves into the conversation. This often goes directly in tandem with low self esteem.

6. **Underlying Trauma or Anxiety:** As Dr. Monique Couvson points out in her work on the experiences of Black girls in schools, many students who struggle with dishonesty may be coping with deep-seated trauma, anxiety, or environmental stressors that make them feel the need to control their narrative—sometimes by lying. For these students, dishonesty can feel like the safest way to navigate a world that feels unpredictable or unsafe.

Supportive Strategies for Addressing Dishonesty

The million-dollar question: What can we do when students lie? While there's no magic fix, there are several supportive strategies that can help create an environment where honesty is encouraged and lying becomes less frequent.

1. **Build a Foundation of Trust:** Establishing a strong, trusting relationship with students is the first step. If students know that they can trust you to be fair and supportive, they're less likely to lie. Kristin Souers and Pete Hall emphasize the importance of creating safe, predictable environments where students feel they can be honest without fear of harsh repercussions. Be consistent, be approachable, and let your students know that you care about them as people, not just as students.

2. **Teach Emotional Regulation and Communication Skills:** Many lies stem from students not knowing how to handle their emotions or communicate their needs effectively. By explicitly teaching emotional regulation and communication skills, we can give students the tools they need to handle tough situations without resorting to dishonesty. Dr. Marc Brackett's RULER approach (Recognizing, Understanding, Labeling, Expressing, and Regulating emotions) is a great framework for helping students understand and manage their feelings.

The RULER Approach

The RULER framework, developed by the Yale Center for Emotional Intelligence, is a research-based approach to teaching emotional intelligence in schools. It stands for Recognizing, Understanding, Labeling, Expressing, and Regulating emotions. These five skills help

(Continued)

> both students and educators build awareness of their emotions, understand their causes and impacts, accurately identify and label emotions, express them appropriately, and manage them effectively. By integrating RULER into the classroom, schools create a supportive environment where students develop the emotional skills necessary for personal growth, healthy relationships, and academic success.

3. **Create a Culture of Mistakes:** Normalize mistakes in your classroom. If students believe that making mistakes is part of the learning process, they'll be less inclined to lie to cover them up. Dr. Lori Desautels emphasizes the importance of creating a brain-friendly classroom where students feel safe to make mistakes and where failure is seen as an opportunity for growth, not something to be feared or hidden.

4. **Give Grace, But Hold Accountability:** When students lie, it's important to hold them accountable in a way that fosters learning and growth, rather than shame. Dr. Ross Greene's collaborative problem-solving approach encourages us to work with students to understand why they lied and to find solutions together. Instead of simply punishing the lie, ask the student what led to the dishonesty and brainstorm ways they can handle similar situations differently in the future.

5. **Focus on the Why, Not Just the What:** When addressing dishonesty, try to dig deeper into the reasons behind the lie. Is the student anxious about something? Are they trying to avoid embarrassment? By addressing the underlying issues, you can help students see that they don't need to lie to protect themselves. Dr. Bruce Perry reminds us that behaviors like lying are often protective mechanisms, and understanding the "why" behind the behavior is key to addressing it effectively.

6. **Model Honesty and Vulnerability:** Kids are watching us all the time, and they learn from our example. Be honest with your students,

even when it's difficult. Admit when you've made a mistake and show them how you handle it. When students see that honesty is valued and that even adults make mistakes, they'll be more likely to follow suit.

7. **Reinforce Positive Behavior:** Catch students being honest, and celebrate it. Positive reinforcement can go a long way in encouraging honesty. Whether it's verbal praise, a note home, or just acknowledging the student's effort to tell the truth, make sure they know that you appreciate their honesty.

8. **Explicitly Teach and Model Empathy:** Empathy can be a great flip side to the behavior of lying and engaging in dishonest actions. When we consider the thoughts and feelings of others, it makes it much harder to lie and be dishonest. Reading books that highlight empathy, use hypothetical scenarios to talk through and role-play, and highlighting real life moments of empathy being shown can help reinforce the importance of this character trait.

Common Challenges in Addressing Dishonesty in the Classroom

Now, let's be real—addressing dishonesty in the classroom is no walk in the park. Even with the best strategies in place, there are some common challenges that teachers face when trying to foster honesty.

1. **Feeling Personally Offended:** It's easy to take it personally when students lie to us. After all, we work hard to create a trusting classroom environment, and when students lie, it can feel like a betrayal. But it's so crucial to remember that it's rarely about you. Students are often lying because they're scared or unsure of how to handle a situation, not because they're trying to disrespect you.

2. **Peer Influence:** Sometimes, students lie because they feel pressure from their peers. This can be tricky to navigate, especially in upper

elementary and middle school grades. Focus on creating a classroom culture where honesty is valued, and help students see that they don't need to lie to fit in.

3. **Balancing Grace and Accountability:** It can be challenging to strike the right balance between giving students grace and holding them accountable for their actions. It's important to remember that we're teaching them life skills, and part of that is learning that honesty matters. But we also need to be empathetic and understand that students are still learning how to navigate complex emotions and situations.

Conclusion

Dishonesty is a tricky one, but with empathy, patience, and the right strategies, we can help our students learn to be more honest, and value honesty. By focusing on the causes and triggers of dishonesty, building trust, and teaching emotional regulation and communication skills, we can create a classroom environment where students feel safe to be truthful.

Behind every lie is a student who's trying to navigate a challenging situation. Let's approach dishonesty with curiosity, understanding, and a commitment to helping our students grow—not just academically, but as people. Character development is the goal, and I guarantee, building honesty as a character trait and a strong value in students really is possible.

Case Study #1

Jonah is a curious 5-year-old boy in Mrs. Anderson's kindergarten class at Hubbard Elementary School. Jonah has many strengths—he's an enthusiastic learner, loves hands-on activities like building with blocks or solving puzzles, and is particularly drawn to any lessons involving science. It's been observed that Jonah has also developed a repeated pattern of dishonesty and sneaky behavior that has become increasingly problematic in the classroom.

Mrs. Anderson, his general education teacher, has made it a point to explicitly teach routines and expectations to the class from the first day of school. In addition, the class participates in weekly social emotional learning (SEL) lessons that focus on themes like empathy, honesty, responsibility, and kindness—values that Mrs. Anderson infuses into daily interactions and weaves into lessons daily. The class has practiced conflict resolution skills, such as how to apologize well and make amends when someone is hurt or upset. Despite these consistent efforts, Jonah continues to engage in dishonest behavior.

Jonah's dishonesty shows up in a variety of ways. For example, during unstructured playtime or recess, Jonah has been observed sneaking toys from the play area into his backpack and engaging in unkind behavior toward peers—such as pushing or taking toys—and then denying it when confronted by teachers or peers. When a classmate tells the teacher that Jonah took their toy or knocked down their building, Jonah will immediately become defensive. He often says, "It wasn't me!" or "I didn't do anything!" This is despite adults or other children witnessing the behavior firsthand. Jonah rarely apologizes or takes accountability for his actions because he will not admit that he has done anything wrong, which leaves conflicts unresolved and feelings hurt.

This pattern of behavior has become a significant barrier to Jonah's social relationships. His peers are beginning to distrust him, and some have started to avoid playing with him during recess or in the classroom. Mrs. Anderson is concerned that if Jonah doesn't learn to take responsibility for his actions, his relationships and overall development could be impacted long-term.

Problem-Solving Approach

Recognizing that Jonah's behavior was becoming a recurring issue, Mrs. Anderson decided to involve other school personnel to address the situation. Rather than view Jonah's behavior as simply "naughty," Mrs. Anderson understood that his dishonesty was likely a reflection of underlying anxiety, fear of getting in trouble, or perhaps even a lack of understanding about the impact of his actions on others. She knew that, just like with any other behavioral challenge, the team would need to get to the root of the problem and design targeted supports to help Jonah.

Mrs. Anderson began documenting Jonah's behavior in different settings—structured classroom activities, unstructured playtime, and recess. She noted that his sneaky behavior and dishonesty were most prevalent during unstructured times when there were fewer immediate consequences for his actions. During teacher-led activities, Jonah was generally cooperative and well-behaved, which suggested that he might have difficulties with impulse control and self-regulation when not under direct supervision.

After collecting data for a couple of weeks, Mrs. Anderson reached out to the school's student support team, which included the school counselor, the behavior interventionist, and Jonah's parents, to schedule a meeting and discuss possible interventions.

Team Collaboration

The initial meeting with the student support team focused on understanding Jonah's behavior and brainstorming solutions. Mrs. Anderson shared her observations and provided documentation of Jonah's behavior, including specific examples of his dishonesty and sneaky behavior. Jonah's parents, Mr. and Mrs. Williams, were concerned about his behavior as well, noting that they had observed similar tendencies at home—particularly when Jonah was caught doing something he wasn't supposed to do, such as sneaking extra snacks or taking his sibling's toys without asking. It was hard for them to hear that this behavior was also shown outside of the home.

The school counselor, Ms. Diaz, brought up an important point: Jonah might be lying and sneaking because he is trying to avoid punishment or feelings of shame. She explained that young children often struggle with the concept of accountability because they fear that admitting to wrongdoing will lead to negative consequences. Instead of acknowledging their mistakes, they lie in an attempt to protect themselves. Ms. Diaz suggested that the team consider focusing on creating a safe space for Jonah to take responsibility without feeling overly punished or shamed.

Mr. Harper, the behavior interventionist, proposed that Jonah's sneaky behavior might also be connected to impulse control issues and suggested that the team implement strategies to help Jonah think through his actions before making unwise choices.

Designing the Intervention

The team decided to design an intervention plan that addressed the root causes of Jonah's behavior while also helping him develop replacement behaviors that were more constructive. They focused on three key goals:

1. Teaching Jonah to recognize and manage his impulses, especially during unstructured times like recess or free play.
2. Creating a safe space for Jonah to take responsibility for his actions without feeling ashamed or punished, emphasizing the importance of honesty and accountability.
3. Strengthening Jonah's ability to repair relationships after conflict, teaching him how to apologize and make amends in a meaningful way.

Components of the Intervention

1. **Social Stories and Visual Supports:** To help Jonah understand the importance of honesty and taking responsibility for his actions, the team decided to use social stories. Social stories are short,

simple narratives that describe specific situations and the appropriate responses. Ms. Diaz created a social story specifically for Jonah about telling the truth, using age-appropriate language and illustrations. The story emphasized that everyone makes mistakes and that it's okay to admit when you've done something wrong. It also highlighted the positive outcomes of being honest, such as maintaining friendships and feeling proud of doing the right thing.

2. **Check-in/Check-out System:** The behavior interventionist, Mr. Harper, suggested implementing a daily check-in/check-out system with Jonah. Each morning, Jonah would check in with Mr. Harper, who would review the expectations for the day and remind Jonah of his goal to practice honesty. Throughout the day, Mrs. Anderson would color in a smiley face, a medium face, or a sad face to show if Jonah showed honest actions during that activity. At the end of the day, Jonah would check out with Mr. Harper to reflect on his behavior, celebrate successes, and create any new goals for the following day. This system would provide Jonah with consistent support and a sense of accountability throughout the day.

3. **Restorative Practices:** To help Jonah repair relationships after conflicts, the team decided to implement structured restorative practices in the classroom. When Jonah had a conflict with a peer, Mrs. Anderson would guide him through a structured process of making amends. This involved having Jonah acknowledge what he had done, express how his actions affected the other person, and work with his peer to find a way to make things right. The focus was on repairing the relationship rather than simply punishing Jonah for his behavior.

4. **Positive Reinforcement and Accountability:** The team decided to use a combination of positive reinforcement and compassionate accountability to encourage Jonah's honesty. When Jonah told the truth or took responsibility for his actions, he would earn a sticker that he added to the front of his take-home folder. However, if Jonah

continued to lie or engage in sneaky behavior, he would not earn the sticker, but would be given the opportunity to reflect on his actions and think about how he could make wiser and more responsible choices next time.

Implementing the Intervention

The intervention was implemented gradually over the course of several weeks. At the start of each day, Jonah would check in with Mr. Harper to go over the day's goals and expectations. During these check-ins, Mr. Harper would remind Jonah to practice honesty and think before acting impulsively. Throughout the day, Mrs. Anderson would prompt Jonah using visual cues as she noticed him becoming frustrated or anxious.

The social stories were read to Jonah regularly, and Mrs. Anderson reinforced their messages by referring back to the stories during moments of conflict or dishonesty. For example, if Jonah denied pushing a classmate during recess, Mrs. Anderson would remind him of the social story about honesty and ask him to think about what the story taught him.

Personalized Support

To ensure that Jonah was receiving personalized support, the team continued to meet regularly to discuss his progress and make any necessary adjustments to the intervention plan. Mr. Harper provided Jonah with additional one-on-one time during recess as needed, helping him practice self-regulation strategies and modeling appropriate social interactions. Ms. Diaz also worked with Jonah during small group sessions, teaching him how to recognize his emotions and communicate them more effectively.

Educating the Class

Mrs. Anderson recognized that addressing Jonah's behavior also required educating the entire class about honesty, accountability, and empathy. She integrated activities targeting these topics into their whole group SEL lessons, encouraging students to think about how their actions affected others and how they could make amends when they made mistakes.

Mrs. Anderson also facilitated class discussions about honesty, using examples from books and videos to illustrate the importance of telling the truth and taking responsibility. These discussions helped create a classroom culture where honesty was valued, and students were encouraged to support one another in making good choices.

Monitoring Progress

The team closely monitored Jonah's progress by tracking his behavior and reflecting on the effectiveness of the intervention. Mr. Harper kept records of Jonah's check-ins and check-outs, noting any improvements in his honesty and impulse control. Mrs. Anderson continued to document Jonah's behavior during both structured and unstructured activities, paying particular attention to how he handled conflicts with his peers.

Initial Challenges

The first few weeks of the intervention were challenging. Jonah continued to struggle with dishonesty, and there were several incidents where he denied engaging in sneaky behavior despite clear evidence to the contrary. Mrs. Anderson and the team remained patient, recognizing that behavioral change would take time and consistency.

Positive Developments

After several weeks, the team began to notice small but significant improvements in Jonah's behavior. He started to make more clear connections to the social story, and there were a few instances where he admitted to making a mistake rather than immediately denying it. Jonah also began to participate more actively in the restorative conversations, showing a willingness to apologize and make amends after conflicts with his peers that they had not yet seen.

Adjustments and Future Steps

Based on Jonah's progress, the team decided to make a few adjustments to the intervention. They increased the amount of positive reinforcement Jonah received for being honest, providing more immediate rewards to reinforce the behavior. Additionally, they incorporated more role-playing activities during Jonah's check-ins with Mr. Harper, allowing Jonah to practice responding to difficult situations in a safe and supportive environment.

Continuous Support

The team recognized that Jonah would need ongoing support to continue building his skills in honesty, accountability, and self-regulation. Mrs. Anderson committed to maintaining restorative practices in the classroom, while Mr. Harper planned to continue the check-in/check-out system for as long as necessary. Ms. Diaz also scheduled regular small group sessions with Jonah to help him further develop his emotional awareness and communication skills.

Conclusion

Jonah's story shows that addressing dishonest behavior is essential to curbing it. Through a combination of empathy, education, and proactive interventions, this can be done in a way that is feasible and meaningful. By focusing on Jonah's underlying needs—such as impulse control, emotional regulation, and fear of punishment—the team was able to create an intervention that not only addressed his behavior but also helped him develop important life skills. Although the journey required patience and persistence, the positive outcomes demonstrated that with the right support, even challenging behaviors like dishonesty can be successfully managed in a way that fosters personal growth and positive relationships.

Case Study #2

Priya is a bright and imaginative second-grader at Columbus Primary School. Her creativity shines during art projects, and she enjoys participating in class discussions where her peers appreciate her thoughtful contributions. Priya's teacher, Ms. Jacobs, has noted that she is a highly social student who has a natural ability to connect with others and is often the first to comfort a classmate who is upset.

However, despite Priya's strengths, Ms. Jacobs has noticed a repeated pattern of dishonesty in the classroom, particularly when it comes to cheating and copying work. Priya often copies her classmates' assignments during independent work time and attempts to cheat during assessments. When confronted about these behaviors, Priya tends to shut down, refusing to speak and avoiding eye contact. This behavior has become more prevalent over the course of the school year, despite the fact that Ms. Jacobs has explicitly taught the class routines, expectations, and the importance of honesty.

Additionally, during unstructured times such as recess, Priya has been observed making unwise choices, such as bending the rules of games or trying to take shortcuts. When approached by teachers or peers about these actions, she again refuses to take accountability for her behavior, shutting down instead of discussing her choices.

To further address the issue, Ms. Jacobs engaged the school counselor, Mrs. Lopez, who has been running weekly social-emotional learning (SEL) lessons for the class. These lessons include themes such as honesty, accountability, and making wise decisions. While Priya actively participates in these lessons, and can speak openly about the importance of these concepts and traits, she has yet to transfer these concepts into her own behavior.

Ms. Jacobs is concerned that Priya's pattern of dishonesty may be rooted in underlying anxieties about her academic performance or fear of failure. Priya appears to struggle with completing tasks independently, and copying work may be her way of avoiding the discomfort of making mistakes. However, without clear accountability and reflection on her actions, Priya is not developing the skills she needs to succeed in the long term.

Problem-Solving Approach

Recognizing that Priya's dishonest behavior was becoming increasingly problematic, Ms. Jacobs decided to initiate a problem-solving approach. She believed that the behavior was not simply a matter of disobedience, but rather an indication that Priya was struggling with underlying emotional or academic difficulties. She knew that these behaviors would likely become more significant and warrant bigger consequences the older she got. Therefore, she decided to involve a broader team of professionals who could collaborate on a more comprehensive intervention plan.

Ms. Jacobs first met with Mrs. Lopez, the school counselor, to discuss potential causes for Priya's behavior. Together, they hypothesized that Priya might be experiencing anxiety around failure or a lack of confidence in her own abilities. Mrs. Lopez also noted that Priya's tendency to shut down when confronted could be a sign that she feels overwhelmed or ashamed, which prevents her from taking responsibility for her actions.

Next, Ms. Jacobs reached out to the assistant principal, Mr. Callahan, who has experience with behavior management and restorative practices. The team agreed that Priya needed additional support to help her develop honesty, accountability, and a stronger sense of self-efficacy. They scheduled a team meeting with Priya's parents, Mr. and Mrs. Patel, to discuss the issue in more depth and to develop a collaborative intervention plan.

Team Collaboration: Developing a Plan

At the team meeting, Ms. Jacobs shared specific examples of Priya's dishonest behaviors, such as copying during independent work and cheating on assessments by hiding her notes on her lap or inside her desk. She also described Priya's pattern of shutting down when confronted about her behavior. Mrs. Lopez contributed her insights from the SEL lessons and shared that Priya appeared to understand the concepts of honesty and accountability in theory but was not yet applying them in her daily actions.

Priya's parents expressed their concern about her dishonesty, noting that they had observed similar behaviors at home, especially when Priya was faced with difficult tasks. Mr. Patel mentioned that Priya often avoided admitting when she had done something wrong, which made it difficult for them to address the behavior constructively. They shared that Priya has an older brother who is in advanced placement and honors classes, and that they share a hope that he will attend a highly esteemed university.

The team agreed that Priya needed targeted support in several key areas: academic confidence, emotional regulation, and accountability. They identified the following goals for Priya:

1. **Develop honesty and accountability:** Priya needs to learn how to take responsibility for her actions and understand the importance of honesty in building trust with others.

2. **Increase academic confidence:** Priya must build her self-efficacy by developing the skills to complete tasks independently, without resorting to copying or cheating.

3. **Improve emotional regulation:** Priya needs effective, tailored strategies to help her manage feelings of anxiety or shame when she is confronted about her behavior.

With these goals in mind, the team worked collaboratively to design an intervention that would support Priya both academically and emotionally.

Designing the Intervention

The intervention plan was designed with a holistic approach, addressing both Priya's academic struggles and her emotional needs. The components of the intervention were as follows:

1. **Explicit Teaching of Honesty and Integrity:** Mrs. Lopez would continue her SEL lessons with an increased focus on honesty and integrity. Priya would be given opportunities to practice honesty in low-stakes situations, such as role-playing scenarios and group discussions. The goal was to help Priya see honesty as a positive behavior that would strengthen her relationships with peers and teachers.

2. **Help-Seeking Strategies:** Ms. Jacobs would implement a "help card" system in the classroom, allowing Priya to discreetly ask for help when she felt uncertain about her work, or if she needed reassurance. This system was designed to give Priya an alternative to cheating or copying by providing her with a way to seek support or encouragement without feeling embarrassed.

3. **Restorative Conversations:** When dishonest behavior occurred, Mrs. Lopez and Mr. Callahan would engage Priya in restorative conversations. These conversations would focus on helping Priya reflect on her actions, acknowledge the impact on others, and make amends. For example, if Priya copied a classmate's work, she would be encouraged to apologize to that classmate and discuss how they could work together more honestly in the future.

4. **Mindfulness and Coping Strategies:** Mrs. Lopez would work with Priya on mindfulness techniques, such as deep breathing and positive self-talk, to help her manage feelings of anxiety or shame. Priya would be encouraged to use these techniques when she felt overwhelmed or tempted to cheat.

Implementing the Intervention

With the intervention plan in place, Ms. Jacobs began implementing the strategies in her classroom. The first step was introducing Priya to the help card system. Ms. Jacobs explained to Priya that if she ever felt unsure about a task, she could place a help card on her desk, and Ms. Jacobs would come over to assist her. This system was designed to empower Priya to ask for help or encouragement without feeling embarrassed or resorting to copying her classmates' work.

Mrs. Lopez continued her SEL lessons, with a renewed focus on honesty and integrity. During these lessons, Priya participated in role-playing activities where she practiced admitting mistakes and discussing how honesty builds trust. These lessons provided Priya with a safe space to explore her feelings about honesty and accountability.

When incidents of dishonesty occurred, Mrs. Lopez or Mr. Callahan would engage Priya in restorative conversations. These conversations were structured to help Priya reflect on her actions, understand the impact on others, and work towards making amends. Priya initially found these conversations difficult, often shutting down and refusing to speak. However, with consistent support and patience from the adults, she gradually began to open up.

In addition to the help card system and SEL lessons, Mrs. Lopez introduced mindfulness exercises to Priya during their individual sessions. Priya was taught how to use deep breathing techniques and positive self-talk to calm herself when she felt anxious or overwhelmed. Over time, Priya began to use these strategies independently, especially during assessments or challenging tasks.

Personalized Support and Educating the Class

To ensure that Priya felt supported throughout the school day, Ms. Jacobs and Mrs. Lopez worked closely together to provide personalized support. Ms. Jacobs checked in with Priya regularly, particularly before assessments or challenging activities, to reassure her that it was okay to ask for help and that she didn't need to copy others' work to succeed.

Mrs. Lopez also worked with Priya's parents to reinforce the intervention at home. They were encouraged to praise Priya for taking responsibility for her actions and to model honesty and accountability in their interactions with her.

In addition to providing personalized support for Priya, Ms. Jacobs made a point of educating the entire class about honesty and integrity. She held class discussions about the importance of doing one's own work and how mistakes are an essential part of the learning process. These discussions helped create a classroom culture where honesty was valued and mistakes were seen as opportunities for growth.

Monitoring Progress

The team monitored Priya's progress through regular check-ins and data collection. Ms. Jacobs kept track of how often Priya used her help cards, engaged in dishonest behavior, and responded to positive reinforcement. Mrs. Lopez also observed Priya during SEL lessons and individual counseling sessions, noting her participation and use of mindfulness techniques.

Every 2 weeks, the team met to review Priya's progress and discuss any necessary adjustments to the intervention. They celebrated Priya's successes, such as her increased willingness to ask for help and her gradual improvement in taking responsibility for her actions.

Initial Challenges

While the intervention showed promise, the team encountered several challenges in the early stages. Priya initially seemed to be using the help cards with reluctance, like she was being forced to do so. It appeared she was still feeling self-conscious about asking for assistance in front of her peers. She continued to shut down during restorative conversations, making it virtually impossible for her to reflect on her actions and move forward.

Additionally, Priya struggled with using mindfulness techniques independently. While she responded well to the exercises during individual sessions with Mrs. Lopez, she found it challenging to apply them in real-time situations, particularly during assessments or moments of high anxiety.

Positive Developments

Despite the initial challenges, the team began to see positive developments after just a few weeks of consistent implementation. Priya became more comfortable using the help card system, and Ms. Jacobs noticed a decrease in the frequency of dishonest behavior during independent work time. Priya also started to open up more during restorative conversations, though she still required gentle prompting from the adults.

One of the most significant positive developments was Priya's increased willingness to take responsibility for her actions. After an incident of copying during a math assessment, Priya approached Ms. Jacobs on her own to admit what she had done. This marked a significant breakthrough, as Priya had previously been unwilling to acknowledge her dishonest behavior, no less bring up a situation of this nature independently.

Adjustments and Future Steps

As the intervention progressed, the team made several adjustments to better meet Priya's needs. To address Priya's discomfort with using help cards in front of her peers, Ms. Jacobs introduced a "quiet signal" that Priya could use to discreetly request help. This modification helped reduce Priya's anxiety and encouraged her to ask for help or reassurance more regularly.

Additionally, Mrs. Lopez continued to work with Priya on mindfulness techniques, focusing on specific strategies that could be easily applied in the classroom. Priya was encouraged to use a breathing exercise called "square breathing" during assessments or challenging tasks, which helped her stay calm and focused.

Continuous Support

The team recognized that supporting Priya's development of honesty and accountability would likely be an ongoing process. Continuous support from Ms. Jacobs, Mrs. Lopez, and Mr. Callahan was essential in helping Priya build the skills and confidence she needed to succeed academically and socially.

The intervention showed promising results, with Priya gradually demonstrating more honesty, accountability, and emotional regulation. While there were still moments of dishonesty and challenges with emotional regulation, the team remained committed to providing Priya with the support and tools she needed to continue making progress.

Conclusion

Priya's story shows the importance of a collaborative, team-based approach to addressing challenging behaviors like dishonesty and cheating in the classroom. When it was shared that Priya's older brother exhibited a lot of academic success, it gave the team more insight into some of the internal pressures Priya may be experiencing that contributed to her behaviors. Without the insight from Priya's parents, this may not have been understood. Through personalized support, explicit teaching of honesty and accountability, and the development of coping strategies, Priya was able to make meaningful strides in overcoming her patterns of dishonest behavior. This also provided a foundation for future teachers to build on as academic pressures resurface in older grades. The success of the intervention highlights the power of patience, persistence, and collaboration in helping students navigate their emotional and academic challenges.

CHAPTER TEN

Bullying

NO MATTER if you're brand new to education or a seasoned professional, bullying is one of those things that makes your heart sink as a teacher. You want your classroom to be a safe, positive space for all students, but then you find out that one student is targeting another with unkind words, exclusion, or even outright aggression. It's frustrating, heartbreaking, and overwhelming. You want to protect the student being bullied, but also help the one doing the bullying change their behavior. It's a tough balance, but here's the good news: with the right strategies, you can address bullying behavior in a way that supports everyone involved.

This chapter is all about breaking down the complexities of bullying, understanding why it happens, and what we can do as teachers to manage it effectively. But first, let's start with some empathy. Managing bullying behavior is not easy. You're not just dealing with hurt feelings—you're navigating power dynamics, social pressures, and often, deeper emotional or psychological issues. The goal is not just to stop the bullying but to create an environment where all students feel safe, respected, and empowered to be themselves. Let's dive in.

Recognizing Bullying as a Barrier to Learning and Engagement

Bullying isn't just a minor issue that gets in the way of learning—it's a serious barrier to engagement for both the students being bullied and the bullies themselves. When a student is being bullied, their focus shifts from learning to survival. They're preoccupied with how to avoid their bully, how to protect themselves, and how to manage their fear and anxiety. For the student doing the bullying, their behavior is also getting in the way of learning. They might be acting out because of something deeper going on in their lives, and the bullying behavior is their way of trying to exert control in an environment where they feel powerless.

We have the also remember that students who engage in bullying behaviors are often dealing with underlying stress or trauma themselves. They may be using bullying as a coping mechanism, trying to gain control in their lives by exerting power over someone else. Understanding this can help us as teachers approach bullying with the right combination of firmness and support.

Causes and Triggers of Bullying Behavior

So why do students bully? There's no one-size-fits-all answer, but there are some common causes and triggers that we see again and again.

1. **Insecurity and Low Self-Esteem:** Many students who bully are struggling with their own feelings of inadequacy. They might bully others to feel more powerful or to mask their own insecurities. Bullying gives them a false sense of control or superiority.

2. **Modeling of Aggressive Behavior:** Sometimes, students who bully have learned these behaviors from the adults or peers around them. If a child is exposed to aggressive behavior—whether it's from

family members, media, or friends—they may mimic that behavior in their own social interactions.

3. **Peer Pressure:** Bullying can also stem from the desire to fit in with a certain group. Students may bully others because they feel pressured by their friends or because they want to gain social status. This is especially true in elementary and middle school when social hierarchies are being established.

4. **Past Trauma or Emotional Distress:** Students who engage in bullying behavior may be dealing with emotional distress or trauma. They might feel powerless in other areas of their lives, and bullying becomes a way to reclaim some control.

5. **Unmet Needs for Attention:** Some students bully because they're desperate for attention. They might feel ignored at home or in the classroom and have learned that bullying is one way to get noticed—even if it's negative attention. At the risk of sounding like a literal broken record, I have to remind us that all behavior has a purpose. For some students, bullying is a maladaptive way of seeking connection or validation.

Supportive Strategies for Addressing Bullying

Addressing bullying isn't about swooping in to punish the bully and protect the victim. It's about creating a literal culture of kindness, accountability, and safety in your classroom. Here are some strategies to get you started:

Build Empathy and Emotional Intelligence

Teaching, reinforcing, and focusing on empathy are some of the most powerful ways to reduce bullying. When students understand how their actions impact others, they're less likely to engage in harmful behaviors. Dr. Marc Brackett emphasizes the importance of teaching emotional intelligence in schools, helping students recognize their own emotions and the emotions of others. You can do this through regular SEL lessons, role-playing activities, and discussions about feelings.

Create opportunities for students to reflect on how their behavior affects others. In morning meetings or circle time, talk about kindness, respect, and understanding. Use books, videos, or real-life examples to show students how empathy can make a difference in someone's day.

Set Clear Expectations and Consequences

By now we fully understand the importance of creating a predictable, consistent environment for students. This includes setting clear expectations for behavior and outlining what will happen if those expectations aren't met. Students need to know that bullying will not be tolerated, but they also need to understand why. When students know the rules and understand the reasoning behind them, they're more likely to follow them.

Make sure your students know what bullying looks like and what the consequences are. More importantly, let them know that if they're struggling with bullying behavior, they can come to you for help. The goal is not to shame or punish but to guide them toward healthy choices.

Teach Problem-Solving Skills

Bullying often stems from students not knowing how to handle conflict or frustration in healthy ways. By teaching problem-solving skills, you give them tools to navigate difficult social situations without resorting to aggression or intimidation. Kristin Souers and Pete Hall emphasize the importance of explicitly teaching students how to resolve conflicts, express their emotions, and negotiate their needs.

Role-play different scenarios where students might feel tempted to bully or be bullied. Practice using "I" statements, like "I feel upset when you tease me," to help students communicate their feelings without escalating the situation.

Foster and Build a Strong Classroom Community

When students feel connected to their peers and to you as their teacher, they're less likely to engage in bullying behavior. Building a strong classroom community means creating opportunities for students to work together, support each other, and build positive relationships.

Try incorporating team-building activities, cooperative learning groups, and buddy systems into your classroom. Encourage students to look out for one another, and praise acts of kindness when you see them.

Foster Open Communication

Students need to know that they can come to you if they're being bullied—or if they're struggling with bullying behavior themselves. Make it clear that your classroom is a safe space where students can talk about their feelings and experiences without fear of judgment.

Encourage students to speak up when they see bullying happening, either by telling an adult or using strategies like standing up for the victim or redirecting the situation. Teach them that being a bystander is not neutral—they have the power to make a difference.

Common Challenges in Addressing Bullying in the Classroom

Addressing bullying is not easy, and there are some common challenges that can make the process even more difficult.

Lack of Honesty from the Bully

Sometimes, students who bully won't admit to their behavior, even when confronted with evidence. This can make it difficult to address the issue head-on. Dr. Monique Couvson reminds us that students who bully often have complex emotional needs, and their dishonesty may be a defense mechanism to protect themselves from further emotional harm.

In these cases, it's important to approach the situation with empathy and patience. Rather than focusing solely on punishment, try to understand what's driving the behavior. Work with the student to reflect on their actions and the impact they've had, and help them come up with ways to make amends.

Bullying Outside of Your Classroom

Bullying doesn't always happen in the classroom—it might occur on the playground, the hallways, in the lunchroom, or online. This can make it harder to monitor and address. Stay connected with other staff members, including recess monitors, lunch aides, and even parents, to get a clearer picture of what's happening when students are outside of your classroom.

Encourage open communication between staff members and involve parents when necessary. Let them know that you're working together to address the issue and that everyone has a role to play in creating a safe environment.

Difficulty Changing Established Patterns

For some students, bullying has become an ingrained behavior that's hard to change. These students might have a history of bullying behavior or have been exposed to aggressive role models. Changing these patterns takes time, consistency, and a lot of patience.

Focus on small wins—celebrate when the student makes a positive choice or shows empathy toward a peer. Keep reinforcing positive behaviors and be patient with the setbacks.

Conclusion

Bullying is a complex issue that requires a multifaceted approach. As teachers, we're not just dealing with behavior in isolation—we're working with students' emotions, histories, and needs. It's challenging, but it's also an incredible opportunity to make a difference in a student's life.

By building empathy, setting clear expectations, teaching problem-solving skills, fostering a strong classroom community, and keeping the lines of communication open, we can create a classroom environment where bullying is addressed proactively and compassionately. Remember, this work takes time, but with consistency and care, you can help your students develop the social–emotional skills they need to thrive—not just in your classroom, but in life.

It's a big job, but I already know that you're more than up for it. Keep going.

Case Study #1

Santino is a second-grade student at Maplewood Elementary School who exhibits many strengths. He is a bright, creative child who enjoys drawing, solving puzzles, and building with blocks. Santino is often enthusiastic during science lessons and enjoys hands-on activities, where he demonstrates both curiosity and focus. When he feels engaged, Santino can be very helpful to his peers, sometimes explaining concepts in his own words or offering to help a classmate who is struggling with an activity.

However, Santino has also developed a repeated pattern of bullying behavior. Despite the strengths he exhibits, particularly in academic and structured environments, Santino struggles significantly during recess, bus rides, and other unstructured times. He targets specific students, engaging in behavior such as taking their belongings, teasing them repeatedly, and excluding them from social activities. His actions have caused distress for multiple classmates, and while his teacher has explicitly taught the class about bullying—focusing on the differences between rudeness, meanness, and bullying—Santino continues to engage in these behaviors.

One of the most concerning aspects of Santino's behavior is that he apologizes when confronted but then repeats the same behavior shortly afterward. His apologies seem to be a learned behavior rather than a genuine expression of remorse or an indication that he understands the impact of his actions. This lack of behavioral change is frustrating for his teachers and school staff, and it suggests that the root causes of Santino's bullying behavior need to be addressed more deeply.

Problem-Solving Approach

The school's response to Santino's bullying behavior was swift, recognizing that his actions were not isolated incidents but part of a larger pattern that required intervention. His general education teacher, Ms. Peterson, first documented the instances of bullying that had occurred in class, during recess, and on the bus. She noted that Santino tended to target a few specific students, engaging in behaviors such as taking their pencils and notebooks, calling them names, and pushing them in line or during play.

When questioned, Santino would often say he was "just joking," but the students on the receiving end did not perceive it that way. On multiple occasions, Santino's actions had led other students to tears and disrupted the class or playtime. Ms. Peterson spoke with Santino about the impact of his behavior and reminded him of the lessons they had covered on the difference between being rude, being mean, and bullying. However, this approach alone did not bring about the desired change.

Recognizing that a more comprehensive approach was needed, Ms. Peterson initiated a collaborative effort to address Santino's behavior. She involved the school counselor, the social worker, the assistant principal, and Santino's parents in the problem-solving process.

Team Collaboration

The team came together for an initial meeting, which included Ms. Peterson (the general education teacher), Ms. Morris (the school counselor), Mr. Alvarez (the social worker), Mr. Simmons (the assistant principal), and Santino's parents, Mr. and Mrs. Rossi. The purpose of this meeting was to gather information, discuss possible root causes of Santino's behavior, and develop a plan to support him in changing his bullying behaviors.

During the meeting, it became clear that Santino had been experiencing some challenges at home. His parents explained that Santino had recently become a big brother and had struggled with the change in attention that came with the arrival of his younger sibling. Mr. and Mrs. Rossi also mentioned that they had noticed an increase in Santino's impulsivity at home, particularly when playing with neighborhood children. He often had difficulty managing frustration and would lash out if things didn't go his way.

The team also noted that Santino's bullying behavior seemed to be triggered most often during unstructured times—such as recess, the bus ride, and free play—when there was less adult supervision and more opportunities for social conflict to arise. It became clear that Santino lacked the skills to navigate these less-structured environments in a healthy way.

Designing the Intervention

Based on the information gathered from the meeting, the team decided to implement a multi-faceted intervention plan aimed at teaching Santino replacement behaviors, improving his emotional regulation skills, and creating a more structured environment during unstructured times.

The intervention plan included the following components:

1. **Check-Ins with the Counselor:** Santino would meet with Ms. Morris, the school counselor, twice a week to work on building empathy, understanding the impact of his actions on others, and practicing emotional regulation strategies. These sessions would focus on role-playing scenarios where Santino would learn and practice appropriate responses to situations that previously led to bullying behavior.

2. **Behavior Contract:** Mr. Simmons, the assistant principal, worked with Santino to develop a behavior contract. This contract outlined specific behaviors that Santino needed to work on, such as

keeping his hands to himself, using kind words, and respecting others' belongings. The contract also included rewards for meeting his behavior goals, such as extra computer time, lunch with a teacher, or positive notes sent home.

3. **Adult Support During Unstructured Time:** Santino was assigned an adult mentor, Mr. Alvarez (the social worker), who would check in with him at the start of recess and the end of recess to help him transition in and out of unstructured times. Mr. Alvarez would also spend some time observing Santino during recess to provide immediate feedback and guidance if he started engaging in bullying behavior.

4. **Social Skills Group:** Santino was placed in a small social skills group facilitated by Ms. Morris. This group, which included a few other students from different classrooms, focused on teaching conflict resolution, communication, and friendship skills. The group met twice a week during lunch to practice these skills in a structured and supportive environment.

5. **Accountability Partner:** As part of the intervention, Santino was paired with an accountability partner—another student in his class who was a positive role model. This student would help Santino stay on track during group activities and free play. The accountability partner's role was not to police Santino's behavior but to provide positive peer influence and encouragement.

6. **Positive Reinforcement:** The intervention plan incorporated a heavy emphasis on positive reinforcement. The team was originally not very keen on the idea of tangible rewards, however, it was noted that Santino was really not ready to be motivated solely by intrinsic motivation. When Santino demonstrated appropriate behavior, whether during structured class time or unstructured recess, he received immediate praise and acknowledgment from teachers and staff. A sticker chart was also implemented, allowing Santino to earn small rewards for meeting his goals.

Implementing the Intervention

Once the intervention plan was designed, the team worked together to implement it with consistency across the school day. Ms. Peterson introduced the behavior contract to Santino in a one-on-one meeting, explaining that it was not a punishment but a way to help him learn and grow. She also explained to Santino that the behavior he was engaging in was bullying, not just being mean or rude. The goal was to name the behavior so that he could better understand the severity of the situation. Santino seemed receptive to the idea of earning rewards for positive behavior, and signed the contract.

Ms. Morris began her twice-weekly check-ins with Santino, starting with a focus on helping him recognize the emotions of others and how his actions impacted his classmates. They worked on role-playing scenarios where Santino practiced using words to express frustration instead of taking someone's belongings or pushing them. Santino struggled with this at first, but Ms. Morris reinforced the lessons with praise when he showed improvement.

Mr. Alvarez started observing Santino during recess, offering guidance when necessary. At the start of each recess, he reminded Santino of his behavior contract and encouraged him to practice the skills he had learned in his check-ins with Ms. Morris. Mr. Alvarez also made sure to point out when Santino played respectfully with others or avoided conflict.

Personalized Support

Recognizing that Santino's bullying behavior often stemmed from his difficulty managing frustration, the team also included personalized supports in the intervention plan. For example, Santino was given access to a designated "calm-down corner" in the classroom, where he could go when he felt overwhelmed. This space included sensory tools, such as stress balls and calming visuals, to help Santino regulate his emotions before they escalated into bullying behavior.

In addition, Ms. Peterson integrated more SEL into her daily routines, reinforcing the lessons that Santino was learning with Ms. Morris. She created opportunities for students to practice kindness and empathy in the classroom, such as "kindness challenges" and group activities that emphasized collaboration and respect for others.

Educating the Class

In addition to working with Santino individually, the team recognized the importance of educating the entire class about bullying. Ms. Peterson led class discussions on kindness, respect, and inclusion. She also revisited the lessons on the difference between being rude, being mean, and bullying, reinforcing that everyone in the class had a role to play in creating a positive environment.

Ms. Peterson also emphasized that students should always come to her or another trusted adult if they were being bullied or witnessed bullying. She emphasized the need for a culture of standing up for one another and being upstanders instead of bystanders.

Monitoring Progress

The team met regularly to monitor Santino's progress. Each week, Ms. Peterson, Ms. Morris, Mr. Alvarez, and Mr. Simmons gathered to review data on Santino's behavior, including reports from recess, bus rides, and classroom interactions. They also reviewed Santino's sticker chart and behavior contract to track his progress toward meeting his goals.

Initial Challenges

As expected, the intervention did not bring about immediate change. In the first few weeks, Santino struggled to break his pattern of bullying behavior. He continued to target the same students during recess and still had trouble managing frustration during group activities. At times,

Santino expressed frustration with the behavior contract, claiming that it was "stupid" and that the contract was making it harder for him.

Despite these challenges, the team remained consistent with the intervention and continued to offer positive reinforcement whenever Santino demonstrated appropriate behavior. They also provided additional support during difficult times, such as giving Santino more frequent breaks in the calm-down corner when he appeared agitated.

Positive Developments

After several weeks of consistent implementation, the team began to notice positive developments in Santino's behavior. He started to show more empathy toward his classmates, occasionally offering to help a peer instead of teasing them. During recess, Mr. Alvarez observed that Santino was more often playing cooperatively with others rather than engaging in bullying behavior.

Santino also began to respond better to his behavior contract. He became more motivated by the rewards and took pride in earning stickers for positive behavior. His social skills group with Ms. Morris also helped him develop better strategies for handling conflict, which he began to apply during unstructured times.

Adjustments and Future Steps

As Santino showed progress, the team adjusted the intervention plan to continue supporting his growth. They reduced the frequency of his check-ins with Mr. Alvarez during recess, allowing Santino more independence while still providing support when needed. They also increased the difficulty of the behavior contract, setting higher goals for Santino as he demonstrated the ability to meet his original goals.

The team continued to monitor Santino's behavior and meet regularly to discuss any further adjustments. They also planned to provide ongoing support for Santino as he continued to develop his social-emotional skills.

Continuous Support

Even as Santino's behavior improved, the team recognized that ongoing support would be essential to maintaining his progress. They planned to continue his participation in the social skills group for the remainder of the school year and scheduled regular check-ins with Ms. Morris to reinforce the lessons he had learned.

Conclusion

Santino's story shows the complexity of addressing bullying behavior in elementary school students. While his initial behavior was concerning, the collaborative approach taken by the school staff, combined with a structured intervention plan, helped Santino begin to change his behavior and develop healthier ways of interacting with his peers. Through consistent support and positive reinforcement, Santino made significant progress, showing that with the right interventions, even the most challenging behaviors can be addressed effectively.

Case Study #2

Nikaylah is a fifth-grade student at Meadowside Elementary School. She has many strengths, including being a highly creative young girl with a deep love for reading. She excels in writing, often crafting compelling stories that captivate her classmates. In structured settings, particularly during language arts classes, she is attentive, engaged, and demonstrates strong leadership skills. Her teachers have noted that she is naturally curious and enjoys intellectual discussions, particularly around topics she is passionate about.

However, despite her many strengths, Nikaylah has a repeated pattern of engaging in bullying behaviors, particularly through cyberbullying. Over the past year, she has been involved in several incidents where she used social media and messaging platforms to target her peers. Her behavior often involves spreading hurtful rumors, excluding classmates from online group chats, and posting unkind comments about her peers.

The school has a strong anti-bullying program, with a special emphasis during October's National Bullying Prevention Month. The entire school explicitly teaches the difference between being rude, being mean, and bullying, and this has been reinforced in classrooms throughout the year. Despite these efforts, Nikaylah continues to engage in bullying behaviors. While she often appears remorseful when confronted and apologizes sincerely, her behavior slows temporarily but typically resurfaces a few months later.

Additionally, her teachers have observed that Nikaylah often makes unwise choices during recess and other unstructured times. She has difficulty managing peer conflicts during these times, and when things do not go her way, she can quickly escalate situations by resorting to bullying tactics, either in person or online.

Problem-Solving Approach

Recognizing that the traditional interventions used so far had not resulted in long-term behavior change, Ms. Johnson, Nikaylah's general education teacher, decided to bring together a team of school personnel to address the issue in a more comprehensive manner. The team included Ms. Johnson, the school counselor, Ms. Alvarez; the assistant principal, Mr. Roberts; the school social worker, Mrs. King; and Nikaylah's parents. The goal of the team was to identify the root causes of Nikaylah's behavior and develop a more individualized intervention plan.

During the initial team meeting, several important pieces of information came to light. First, Nikaylah's parents shared that she is adopted and has been struggling with her identity as one of the few Black students in her predominantly white school. This year, she had started reconnecting with members of her birth family, an experience that has been both exciting and stressful for her. While she had expressed happiness about meeting her birth relatives, she was also dealing with confusion, anxiety, and questions about her identity. Her adoptive parents shared that they had noticed increased tension at home, particularly around issues related to race and adoption.

The team realized that these underlying emotional and social factors could be major contributors to Nikaylah's bullying behavior. Ms. Alvarez, the school counselor, noted that children who feel marginalized or who are struggling with their identity sometimes lash out at others as a way to gain control or assert power. In Nikaylah's case, the use of cyberbullying may have been a way for her to assert dominance and feel a sense of control in her peer group, especially when she was feeling vulnerable or uncertain about her own place in the world.

Team Collaboration

The team agreed that a multi-faceted approach was needed to address both the behavior and the underlying emotional issues contributing to it. They recognized that Nikaylah needed support not only in learning how to change her behavior but also in navigating the complex emotions she was experiencing related to her adoption, her racial identity, and her reconnection with her birth family.

The school counselor, Ms. Alvarez, suggested that the family consider outside therapy to provide additional emotional support for Nikaylah. Her adoptive parents agreed that therapy could be beneficial and were in the process of seeking a therapist who specialized in adoption and identity issues. The school team also offered to communicate directly with the therapist to ensure that the work being done in therapy could be reinforced in the school environment. Mrs. King, the social worker, volunteered to be the point of contact for the therapist and to provide updates on Nikaylah's behavior and progress at school.

Designing the Intervention

Based on the information gathered during the team meetings, the group designed an intervention plan that targeted both the bullying behaviors and the underlying emotional challenges that seemed to be fueling them. The intervention plan included the following components:

1. **Weekly Check-Ins with the Counselor:** Nikaylah would meet with Ms. Alvarez once a week for individual counseling sessions. These sessions would focus on helping her process her feelings around her adoption, her racial identity, and her reconnection with her birth family. The sessions would also address the impact of bullying on her peers and help her develop empathy and conflict resolution skills.

2. **Digital Citizenship and Social Media Education:** Given that much of the bullying was happening online, the school's technology teacher, Ms. Carter, agreed to work with Nikaylah on digital citizenship lessons. These lessons would focus on responsible use of technology, the impact of cyberbullying, and strategies for managing online interactions in a positive and respectful way.

3. **Behavior Contract:** Mr. Roberts, the assistant principal, worked with Nikaylah to develop a behavior contract. This contract outlined specific goals related to reducing bullying behaviors and making more positive choices during recess and unstructured times. The contract also included clear consequences for continued bullying and rewards for meeting her behavior goals, such as extra free time, special privileges, or positive notes home.

4. **Mentorship Program:** Mrs. King, the social worker, arranged for Nikaylah to participate in a mentorship program with an older student. The mentor, a sixth-grade girl who had also experienced adoption and identity struggles, would meet with Nikaylah once a week during lunch. The goal of the mentorship was to provide her with a positive role model and a safe space to talk about her feelings and experiences.

5. **Increased Supervision During Unstructured Time:** To prevent further incidents of bullying during recess and other unstructured times, the school increased adult supervision during these periods.

Ms. Johnson, the general education teacher, also worked with the recess monitors to ensure that they were aware of the specific triggers and dynamics that led to bullying incidents so they could intervene more effectively.

Components of the Intervention

The intervention plan focused on both addressing the immediate bullying behavior and providing long-term emotional support. The key components were:

- **Counseling and Emotional Support:** Weekly counseling sessions with the school counselor allowed Nikaylah to process her complex emotions in a safe and supportive environment.
- **Behavior Monitoring and Accountability:** The behavior contract and increased supervision during unstructured times provided clear expectations and consequences for bullying behavior while also giving Nikaylah the opportunity to earn rewards for positive behavior.
- **Digital Literacy Education:** Lessons on digital citizenship helped address the specific issue of cyberbullying and gave Nikaylah tools for managing online interactions responsibly, as well as educating her on the concept of a digital footprint and consequences to unsafe online behavior.
- **Mentorship and Peer Support:** The mentorship program provided a positive peer role model who could relate to some of the challenges Nikaylah was facing.

Implementing the Intervention

Once the intervention plan was finalized, the team began implementing it with consistency across the school day. Ms. Alvarez began her weekly check-ins with Nikaylah, focusing first on building trust and rapport. She used these sessions to help Nikaylah explore her feelings about her adoption and her reconnection with her birth family, as well as to talk about the impact her bullying behavior was having on her peers. Ms. Alvarez also used role-playing and other activities to help Nikaylah practice conflict resolution skills and develop more empathy for others.

Ms. Carter started her digital citizenship lessons with Nikaylah, emphasizing the importance of respectful online communication and the consequences of cyberbullying. Together, they discussed scenarios where negative online behavior could escalate, and Ms. Carter helped Nikaylah brainstorm strategies for handling online conflicts in a more positive way.

The behavior contract was implemented immediately, and Mr. Roberts monitored Nikaylah's progress closely. Ms. Johnson communicated regularly with the recess monitors to ensure they were aware of potential triggers and could intervene before bullying incidents occurred.

Personalized Support

To further support her, the team also provided personalized support tailored to her specific needs. For instance, Ms. Johnson allowed her to have a quiet corner in the classroom where she could go when she felt overwhelmed or frustrated. This gave her a safe space to calm down and regroup before rejoining her peers. Additionally, Ms. Johnson worked on building a stronger relationship with Nikaylah by offering her more opportunities to share her thoughts and feelings during class discussions, helping her feel valued and heard.

Educating the Class

Recognizing that bullying is not just an individual problem but a community issue, the school also took steps to educate the entire class about bullying. Ms. Johnson led class discussions on the impact of bullying and the importance of kindness and inclusion. She also used the opportunity to revisit the lessons from the school's anti-bullying program, reminding students of the differences between being rude, being mean, and engaging in bullying behavior.

Mr. Roberts held an assembly for the entire fifth grade on digital citizenship, with a specific focus on the responsible use of social media and online communication. The assembly aimed to help all students become more aware of the impact their online behavior can have on their peers. The students signed a collective agreement, like a pledge, about safe online behavior.

Monitoring Progress

The team regularly monitored Nikaylah's progress by checking in with her, observing her interactions with her peers, and reviewing her behavior contract. They met biweekly to discuss her behavior, share updates, and make any necessary adjustments to the intervention plan.

Initial Challenges

Despite the comprehensive intervention plan, the team faced initial challenges in getting Nikaylah to fully engage with the process. At times, she resisted the counseling sessions, claiming that she didn't need to talk about her feelings. She also struggled with consistency in following her behavior contract, often meeting her goals for a few days and then slipping back into old patterns. Nikaylah shared that she viewed herself as someone who was a bully, and was mean, and that she felt stuck in that being a core part of her social identity. This revelation encouraged the team to remain patient and consistent in their approach, reinforcing positive behavior and gently encouraging her to continue participating in the interventions, and really focusing on positive reinforcement, and highlighting her strengths as a friend and a citizen.

Positive Developments

After a few months, the team began to notice positive changes in Nikaylah's behavior. She started to engage more meaningfully in the counseling sessions and began using some of the conflict resolution skills she had learned.

Incidents of cyberbullying decreased significantly, and she began to use her online platforms more responsibly. The behavior contract became an effective tool for helping her stay accountable for her actions, and she began to take more ownership of her behavior during unstructured times.

Adjustments and Future Steps

As Nikaylah's behavior improved, the team made adjustments to her intervention plan. They reduced the frequency of her check-ins with Mr. Roberts and gradually increased her responsibilities in the classroom and during recess. They also worked with her parents and outside therapist to ensure that the emotional support she was receiving at school was reinforced at home and in her new weekly therapy sessions.

Continuous Support

Moving forward, the team recognized the importance of providing ongoing support for Nikaylah as she continued to navigate her identity and peer relationships. They planned to continue her participation in the social skills group and to offer periodic check-ins with Ms. Alvarez to ensure that she had a safe space to process her emotions.

Conclusion

Nikaylah's situation shows that when we address bullying behavior, we almost always find that it's tied to deeper emotional struggles. While the road to change was not always smooth, the collaborative efforts of the school team, combined with consistent support and a personalized intervention plan, helped Nikaylah begin to make meaningful progress. By addressing both the behavior and the underlying emotional issues, the team was able to support her in developing healthier ways of interacting with her peers, seeing herself, and managing her emotions.

CHAPTER ELEVEN

The Elephant in the Room

TEACHING CAN be one of the most rewarding professions in the world, but it's also one of the most demanding. Here we are: expected to not only deliver content in meaningful ways but also to manage a classroom full of diverse needs, personalities, and behaviors. This becomes even more challenging when you have students exhibiting disruptive or challenging behaviors. It can feel like you're fighting a losing battle every day—balancing your lesson plans, trying to meet academic standards, and simultaneously putting out behavioral fires.

Let's be real—managing challenging behavior can be exhausting. It's physically, mentally, and emotionally draining, and it can often leave you feeling overwhelmed, defeated, and on the edge of burnout. You're not alone if you feel this way, and it's important to acknowledge the elephant in the room. The toll of managing these behaviors goes beyond just "being teacher tired." We're talking about serious impacts on your well-being, and it's critical that we address this, because you can't pour from an empty cup.

The Impact of Vicarious Trauma

The concept of vicarious trauma refers to the emotional and psychological toll that comes from being exposed to the trauma and suffering of others, even if you're not the one directly experiencing it yourself. Teachers, especially those working with students who have experienced trauma or have significant behavioral needs, are particularly vulnerable to vicarious trauma. Dr. Lori Desautels explains that when teachers are constantly managing trauma-induced behaviors, they can start to experience symptoms similar to those of the students themselves: anxiety, stress, fatigue, and emotional exhaustion.

When you're working with students who have been through traumatic experiences, their behaviors are often a reflection of their internal struggles. Aggression, defiance, withdrawal, and emotional dysregulation are often their way of communicating their pain and distress. If you've made it this far, I already know that you care deeply about students, and want to help them—so you take on their emotional burdens, whether you fully realize it or not. Dr. Bruce Perry's research on childhood trauma emphasizes that when teachers witness or experience the aftermath of student trauma day in and day out, it can lead to burnout, compassion fatigue, and vicarious trauma.

This isn't just about the big, dramatic moments either. It's also about the accumulation of small, daily stressors: the constant disruptions, the unpredictability of outbursts, the emotional labor of trying to keep the peace, the lack of time to regroup between incidents, and the pressure to maintain a "calm and collected" demeanor. These moments pile up and, before you know it, you're feeling worn out and defeated.

Kristin Souers and Pete Hall highlight that teachers must recognize the emotional toll that comes with supporting students in crisis. This toll can morph into exhaustion, emotional detachment, or even physical symptoms like headaches, sleep disturbances, and muscle tension. It's vital to address this vicarious trauma to ensure that teachers remain effective and emotionally healthy.

Taking Care of Basic Needs

We know the importance of teaching students to take care of themselves—whether it's reminding them to drink water, take brain breaks, or even use the restroom. But how often do we actually practice what we preach? When you're in the trenches of managing challenging behavior, it's all too easy to forget about your own basic needs. You're likely skipping lunch, holding off bathroom breaks, and pushing through the day without giving yourself the necessary downtime to recharge.

We need to embody the idea that self-care isn't just a buzzword; it's a necessity. If you're not meeting your own basic needs, you can't expect to be emotionally regulated or patient enough to manage a room full of kids—especially those with challenging behaviors. When your body and brain are deprived of nourishment, rest, and hydration, you're much more likely to be reactive, which can escalate situations rather than de-escalate them.

When you're exhausted and running on empty, you're not able to be the best version of yourself for your students. We've all been there—feeling irritable and short-tempered, unable to muster up the energy to respond calmly when a student acts out. This is why taking care of your basic needs is so essential. It's not selfish; it's necessary. You need to give yourself permission to prioritize your own well-being. Keep a water bottle on hand, pack healthy snacks, set boundaries for when you can take a short break (even if it's just for a few minutes), and ensure that you're getting enough sleep at night. Your students need a regulated, present teacher, and that means you need to take care of yourself first.

Tapping Out: Knowing When to Ask for Help

There's a myth in education that teachers are supposed to be superheroes who can handle anything and everything on their own. Let's debunk that right now: you do not have to do this alone. It's okay to ask for help, and in fact, it's necessary. When you're managing students with significant behavior challenges, it's essential to recognize your limits and know when to tap out.

Dr. Monique Couvson, who focuses on the educational experiences of marginalized students, advocates for the idea that teachers need systemic and community support. No teacher should feel like they are solely responsible for solving every behavioral challenge in their classroom. The "tap out" strategy, where teachers can step away to take a break when they feel overwhelmed, is a helpful way to prevent burnout and maintain emotional balance. This could involve asking a colleague to cover your class for a few minutes while you take a breather, or having a designated support staff member step in when a particular student's behavior escalates.

Pete Hall and Kristin Souers stress the importance of collegial support. They argue that teachers need to work together to create a culture of collaboration and mutual support. When a teacher is dealing with a challenging situation, it should be normalized to ask for help rather than viewed as a sign of weakness. Whether it's stepping out of the classroom to take a moment for yourself or tapping into your support system to get advice or even hands-on help, knowing when to tap out is an essential self-care strategy. You cannot—and should not—carry the weight of these challenges alone.

Common Challenges in Addressing Exhaustion

Managing challenging behavior is hard, and part of that difficulty comes from the emotional labor involved in staying patient, compassionate, and engaged. Teachers are often juggling so many responsibilities that adding the emotional and physical toll of managing behavior can feel overwhelming. Let's talk about some of the common challenges that come with addressing this exhaustion.

1. **Feeling Guilt or Shame for Needing Help:** Many teachers feel guilty when they aren't able to handle everything on their own. There's a pervasive narrative in education that "good" teachers are those who can do it all. But the truth is, no one can. Acknowledging when you need help isn't a sign of weakness; it's a sign of wisdom. It's about knowing your limits and advocating for what you need to be the best teacher you can be.

2. **Dealing with External Pressures:** Teachers are under constant pressure from administration, community, parents, and even themselves to produce academic results. When you're spending significant time and energy managing behavior, it can feel like you're failing to meet those expectations. This pressure can add to the exhaustion, making it feel like there's never enough time or energy to do everything that's being asked of you.

3. **The Emotional Toll of Compassion Fatigue:** Compassion fatigue is a real phenomenon. Dr. Lori Desautels explains that compassion fatigue occurs when educators spend so much emotional energy caring for their students that they end up feeling drained and depleted. It's the burnout that comes from giving too much of yourself without replenishing your own emotional reserves. When you're constantly giving to your students, especially those with high needs, it's easy to lose sight of your own emotional well-being.

4. **Balancing Self-Care with Classroom Responsibilities:** It's easy to talk about self-care, but finding the time and space for it in the middle of a busy school day can be a real challenge. Teachers are often so focused on their students' needs that they forget to take care of their own. Finding that balance—where you're meeting your students' needs but also prioritizing your own well-being—can be incredibly tricky.

Supportive Strategies for Addressing Exhaustion

So, how do we manage this? How do we navigate the constant exhaustion that comes with managing challenging behavior, while also doing what's best for our students and ourselves?

1. **Build a Support Network:** You need a strong support system of colleagues, administrators, and support staff who can step in when you need a break. Don't be afraid to ask for help—whether it's asking for a moment to step out of the classroom or seeking advice on how to handle a specific situation. You don't have to be a superhero; you just have to be human.

2. **Create a Routine for Self-Care:** Incorporate self-care into your daily routine. This might mean setting aside five minutes in the morning for deep breathing, making sure you eat a healthy snack, or taking a brief walk during lunch. Even small acts of self-care can have a big impact on your ability to manage stress.

3. **Practice Mindfulness and Emotional Regulation:** Dr. Marc Brackett's work emphasizes the importance of emotional intelligence for teachers. Practice mindfulness techniques, such as deep breathing or grounding exercises, to help you stay calm and centered in moments of stress. The more you can regulate your own emotions, the more effectively you'll be able to help your students regulate theirs.

4. **Take Breaks When You Need Them:** Give yourself permission to step away when things get overwhelming. Whether it's stepping out of the classroom for a few minutes or taking a mental health day when needed, taking breaks is a crucial part of maintaining your emotional health.

5. **Be Compassionate with Yourself:** Lastly, be kind to yourself. You are doing incredibly hard work, and it's okay to feel overwhelmed at times. Remind yourself that you're human and that it's okay to have moments where you don't have all the answers.

Conclusion

Managing challenging behavior is one of the toughest aspects of teaching, and it's okay to admit that it's exhausting. The emotional labor involved in supporting students, especially those with significant behavioral needs, takes a real toll. Recognizing the impact of vicarious trauma, meeting your own basic needs, and knowing when to ask for help are all essential steps in maintaining your well-being as an educator. By taking care of yourself, you're not only preserving your own health, but you're also modeling the kind of emotional regulation and self-care that will benefit your students in the long run.

As Dr. Bruce Perry says, "Relationships are the agents of change, and the most powerful therapy is human love." Remember to extend that love and compassion to yourself, too.

Acknowledgments

This book has been both a whirlwind and labor of love, and there are many individuals I have to give a sincere thanks to. I am forever grateful for the expertise of Sam Ofman and Navin Vijayakumar for their truly invaluable assistance in navigating the world of "grown-up books." Thank you for believing in me and the power of teachers supporting other teachers.

This work would not have been possible without the years of experience working alongside other dedicated and incredible educators who have shaped my path in the field. You have taught me endless lessons just by compassionately teaching children.

All of the brilliantly creative, feisty, passionate, and deserving students I have taught over the years: this book is for you, and from you! Every problem-solving conversation, "think sheet," and crisis call has built my toolbox so I can be who I am today. Never change!

And of course, my beautiful family! Thank you to my husband for all the park trips and ice cream adventures you took with the kids so I could have some focused time to plan, research, and write. You're my better half. To my rambunctious and adorable kids, who provided so much joy amidst the tedious writing process, you are my whole world. Thanks for being you.

About the Author

Allison (Allie) Szczecinski is a seasoned special education teacher and author from Chicago, Illinois. She has a bachelor's degree in Special Education from Illinois State University and a master's degree in Special Education from The University of Illinois. After starting her career in self-contained special education classrooms in Chicago, Allie began sharing her self-made resources along with tips and tricks for teachers through the online platform Miss Behavior. She runs a popular Instagram channel (instagram.com/_missbehavior), writes for her weekly blog (www.missbehaviorblog.com), and sells a host of resources to support students' social, emotional, and behavioral health (http://bit.ly/missbehaviortpt). Allie is the author of the children's book *Roaring Mad Riley*. She currently resides in Chicago with her husband, adorable children, and two active rescue dogs.

References

Bernstein, G. A., & Garfinkel, B. D. (2017). *School refusal: Assessment and intervention within school settings.* Professional Resource Exchange.

Brackett, M. A. (2019). *Permission to feel: Unlocking the power of emotions to help our kids, ourselves, and our society thrive.* Celadon Books.

Burke Harris, N. (2018). *The deepest well: Healing the long-term effects of childhood adversity.* Houghton Mifflin Harcourt.

Couvson, M. (2016). *Pushout: The criminalization of Black girls in schools.* The New Press.

Delahooke, M. (2019). *Beyond behaviors: Using brain science and compassion to understand and solve children's behavioral challenges.* PESI Publishing & Media.

Desautels, L. (2020). *Connections over compliance: Rewiring our perceptions of discipline.* Wyatt-MacKenzie Publishing.

Dweck, C. S. (2006). *Mindset: The new psychology of success.* Random House.

Fisher, A. V., Godwin, K. E., & Seltman, H. (2014). Visual environment, attention allocation, and learning in young children: When too much of a good thing may be bad. *Psychological Science, 25*(7), 1362–1370. https://doi.org/10.1177/0956797614533801

Glad, D., Silverman, W. K., & Kearney, C. A. (2013). *Anxiety disorders in children and adolescents: Research, assessment, and intervention.* The Guilford Press.

Greene, R. W. (2008). *Lost at school: Why our kids with behavioral challenges are falling through the cracks and how we can help them.* Scribner.

Greene, R. W. (2014). *The explosive child: A new approach for understanding and parenting easily frustrated, chronically inflexible children* (5th ed.). HarperCollins.

Heyne, D., Sauter, F. M., Van Widenfelt, B. M., Vermeiren, R., & Westenberg, P. M. (2011). School refusal and anxiety in adolescence: Theoretical and empirical considerations.

Clinical Child and Family Psychology Review, 14(2), 92–107. https://doi.org/10.1007/s10567-011-0082-5

Kearney, C. A., & Graczyk, P. A. (2014). A response to intervention model for school refusal behavior. *Behavioral Disorders, 39*(4), 257–268. https://doi.org/10.1177/019874291403900405

Kearney, C. A., & Silverman, W. K. (1995). Family involvement in school refusal behavior: A comparison of families of adolescents with school attendance problems. *Journal of Clinical Child Psychology, 24*(1), 14–23. https://doi.org/10.1207/s15374424jccp2401_3

Perry, B. D. (2006). Fear and learning: Trauma-related factors in the adult education process. *New Directions for Adult and Continuing Education, 110,* 21–27. https://doi.org/10.1002/ace.215

Perry, B. D., & Szalavitz, M. (2017). *The boy who was raised as a dog: And other stories from a child psychiatrist's notebook* (Updated ed.). Basic Books.

Perry, B. D., & Winfrey, O. (2021). *What happened to you?: Conversations on trauma, resilience, and healing.* Flatiron Books.

Siegel, D. J., & Bryson, T. P. (2016). *The whole-brain child: 12 revolutionary strategies to nurture your child's developing mind.* Bantam.

Souers, K., & Hall, P. (2016). *Fostering resilient learners: Strategies for creating a trauma-sensitive classroom.* ASCD.

Venet, A. S. (2021). *Equity-centered trauma-informed education.* W. W. Norton & Company.

Wlodkowski, R. J. (1983). *Enhancing adult motivation to learn: A comprehensive guide for teaching all adults.* Jossey-Bass.

Index

Page numbers followed by *f* refer to figures.

A

Academic confidence, 197
Accommodations:
    for anxiety, 111–112, 126
    for back talk, 34
    in classrooms, 49, 50, 126
    flexibility in, 111–112, 125
    for inattention, 157, 158
    for neurological conditions, 158
    for school refusal treatment, 42, 44, 49, 50
Accountability. *See also* Responsibility
    and behavior monitoring, 220
    for bullying, 205, 223
    continuous support for, 202
    description of, xiii
    and dishonesty, 185, 188
    education about, 192
    emotional check-ins for, 191
    and grace, 185, 187
    partners for, 212
    positive reinforcement for, 191–192, 200
    reactive strategies for, 46
    restorative practices for, 24
    safe spaces for, 190, 199
    SEL lessons for, 195–197
    support for, 194
Active listening, 84, 139. *See also* Respectful communication
ADHD, xiii, 86, 157, 158
Affirmation cards, 43*f*, 109, 116
Affirmations, 10, 42, 109, 113
Aggression, 133–158
    addressing, 136–139
    and back talk, 25
    as barrier to learning, 134
    bullying as, 203–206, 208
    case studies of, 140–158
    causes of, 134–136
    challenges of, 139–140
    cues for, 143, 152, 153

Aggression (*continued*)
  dealing with, xii, 226
  Desautels on, 134, 137, 139
  description of, xiii
  from emotional dysregulation, 135
  emotional regulation of, 137, 150
  exercises for, 144
  from fear, 135
  Greene on, 135, 138
  and hypervigilance, 149
  intervention plans for, 137–138
  and isolation, 140
  PE activities for, 152
  from peer conflicts, 136
  peer mediation for, 152
  Perry on, 134
  and predictability, 137
  SEL techniques for, 138–139, 145
  from sensory overload, 135
  from unmet needs, 135
Aggressive behavior:
  behavior intervention plans for, 138
  in bullies, 204–205
  causes of, 149
  education on, 153
  escalation of, 148
  from fear, 135
  forms of, 134
  problem-solving approach to, 141
  routines for, 137
  teams for, 137–138, 142, 147
Anxiety, 105–131
  accommodations for, 49
  addressing, 107–113
  affirmations for, 109
  and aggression, 135, 137, 149
  assessment of, 45
  and back talk, 18
  as barrier to learning, 105–106
  bibliotherapy for, 112
  breathing exercises for, 109–111, 110*f*
  from bullying, 204, 217
  calm spaces for, 108–109
  choice boards for, 76
  coping skills for, 42, 51, 112–113, 126, 198, 201
  Desautels on, 105, 108
  description of, xii, xiii
  and dishonesty, 183, 189, 196–197
  and disruptive behavior, 86, 97
  distractions for, 112
  and elopement, 3, 6, 7, 52
  emotional check-ins for, 22, 111–112
  -friendly classrooms, 113
  Greene on, 112
  from helplessness, 75
  and inattention, 157, 159
  manifestations of, 106–107
  Perry on, 107, 110, 111
  and predictability, 64–65
  reduction strategies for, 53
  rise of, x
  and school refusal, 37
  separation, 39, 98–99
  social, 38, 48
  structure for, 108

support for, 40, 50, 53, 55
  of teachers, 226
  2 × 10 strategy for, 56–57
Anxiety cycles, 112
Assessment methods, 44–45, 106, 195, 197, 199–201
Attendance:
  and back talk, 30, 32, 34
  flexibility in, 45, 46
  and school refusal, 38, 46, 47, 49, 56
  short daily, 54
Attention-seeking behaviors, 100

B
Back talk, 17–35
  case studies of, 25–035
  Desautels on, 17, 20
  description of, xi
  emotional check-ins for, 21–23
  Greene on, 18–19, 23
  managing, 20–24
  replacement behavior for, 20–21, 32
  restorative practices for, 23–25
  toolbox for addressing, 18–19
Behavior contracts, 211, 213–215, 219–223
Behavior Intervention Plans (BIPs), 138
Behavior management strategies, 84–85
Behavior monitoring, 220
Behavior replacement plans (BRPs), 20–21, 91
Bibliotherapy, 112

Brackett, Marc:
  on anxiety, x, 106
  on disruptive behavior, 85
  on elopement, 18
  on emotion labeling, 10
  on emotional check-ins, 111
  on emotional regulation, 162, 230
  on empathy, 18, 205
  mood meter of, 22
  on perfectionism, 183
  on predictability, 19, 137
  RULER framework of, 84, 184
  on school refusal, 37–38
Brain breaks, 5, 108, 227
Brain training, 64f
BrainPOP, 45
Break cards, 4, 143, 144, 146
Breathing exercises. *See also* Grounding exercises; Mindfulness
  for aggression, 137, 143, 144
  for anxiety, 109–111, 110f, 113, 121, 126
  in calm corners, 10, 32
  for dishonesty, 199
  for disruptive behavior, 92, 94
  for emotional regulation, 100–101, 116, 150
  for helplessness, 77
  for inattention, 169
  and mindfulness, 42, 117, 127–128, 137, 198, 201
  reminders for, 152–153
  safe spaces for, 162

Breathing exercises (*continued*)
  in social work sessions, 55
  square, 201
  for teachers, 230
  teaching, 129
Breathing mats, 110*f*
BRPs (behavior replacement plans), 20–21, 91
Bullying, 203–224
  as barrier to learning, 204
  causes of, 204–205
  challenges of, 207–208
  and classroom communities, 207
  cyber-, 216, 218–221, 223
  description of, xiii
  emotional intelligence for, 205–206
  empathy-building for, 205–206
  established patterns in, 208–209
  expectation-setting for, 206
  open communication for, 207
  outside classrooms, 208
  problem-solving skills for, 206
  strategies for, 205–207
Burke-Harris, Nadine, 109
Burnout, 83, 87, 139–140, 225, 226, 228, 229. *See also* Exhaustion; Teacher stress

C

Calm down cards, 101–103
Calm down corners, 137–138, 143–147, 213, 215. *See also* Relaxation spaces
Calm down kits, 92–94, 100
Calm down strategies, 32, 33
Calm spaces, 108–109
CASEL (Collaborative for Academic and Social Emotional Learning), 139. *See also* Social Emotional Learning (SEL)
Check-in/check-out system, 191
Check-ins, *see* Emotional check-ins
Class clown behavior, 82, 97, 99, 100, 102
Classroom charters, 84
Classroom communities, 23, 50, 207, 209
Collaborative for Academic and Social Emotional Learning (CASEL), 139. *See also* Social Emotional Learning (SEL)
Compassion fatigue, 226, 229
Compliance, 82, 105, 107
Conflict resolution:
  in aggression, 145
  for bullying, 219, 221, 222
  classroom instruction on, 152, 153–154, 212
  for dishonesty, 188
  in elopement, 14
  for inattention, 179
  peer leadership for, 155
  replacement behaviors for, 150–151
Consequences:
  in behavior contracts, 219
  of bullying, 220, 221
  of dishonesty, 182, 189, 190, 196

of disruption, 83
expectations of, 84, 206
fear of, 182
of impulsive behavior, 173, 175
inconsistent application of, 87
problem-solving conversations vs., 19
restorative circles vs., 19
stop and think strategy for, 176
Consistency, *See* Predictability; Routines; Structured environments
Coping skills:
for aggression, 135
for anxiety, 112–113, 124, 126, 129
counseling for, 12
for elopement, 13
for emotional dysregulation, 135
for inattention, 159
for school refusal treatment, 44
teaching, 42, 112–113, 121
toolbox for, 113, 116, 119–120, 159
Couvson, Monique, 135, 138, 163, 183, 207, 228
Culture of mistakes, 185
Cyberbullying, 216, 218–221, 223. *See also* Bullying

D

Defiance:
from anxiety, 107, 113
back talk as, 17–18
behavior replacement for, 20–21
causes of, x
as communication, 141
as disruptive behavior, 82
from feedback, 26
and inattention, 157
restorative practices for, 24
strategies for, 19, 22
from trauma, 226
Delahooke, Mona, 82–83, 85, 86
Desautels, Lori:
on aggression, 134, 137, 139
on anxiety, 105, 108
on back talk, 17, 20
on communication, x
on compassion fatigue, 229
on dishonesty, 182, 185
on disruptive behavior, 82, 84
on elopement, 2, 5, 6
on emotional check-ins, 22
on helplessness, 60, 62
on inattention, 158
on mindfulness, 42
on school refusal, 38, 40
on self-care, 87
Digital citizenship, 219–222
Digital literacy education, 220
Dishonesty, 181–202
for attention, 183
as barrier to learning, 181–182
of bullies, 207
case studies of, 187–202
causes of, 182–183
challenges of, 186–187
consequences of, 182
Desautels on, 182, 185
description of, xiii

Dishonesty (*continued*)
   Greene on, 154, 185, 201
   from low self-esteem, 183
   and perfectionism, 183
   Perry on, 182, 185
   and responsibility avoidance, 183
   RULER approach to, 184–185
   strategies for, 184–186
   from trauma, 183
Disruptive behavior, 81–104
   and aggression, 133, 134, 141, 144, 148
   and anxiety, 105, 111
   as barrier to learning, 81–82
   behavior management studies for, 84
   Brackett on, 85
   and bullying, 210
   calm corners for, 11
   case studies of, 88–104
   challenges of, 86–87
   consequences of, 83
   defining, 82–83
   Desautels on, 82, 84
   description of, xii
   and dishonesty, 181
   effect on teachers, 225–226
   emotional check-ins for, 22
   forms of, 82
   and inattention, 160, 165, 167
   managing, 84–86
   Perry on, 83, 86, 158
   redirection of, 85
   sensory supports for, 175
   student engagement for, 85–86
Distractions, 91, 92, 112, 158, 160, 170
Distractive behavior:
   aggression as, 133
   as disruption, 82, 85, 88
   as helplessness, 73, 75, 77
Downstairs brain, 145
Dweck, Carol, 63
Dysregulation, x, 81–82, 99–101, 158

E
EBDs (Emotional behavioral disorders), 52
Elopement, 1–16
   addressing, 4–5
   Brackett on, 18
   case studies of, 8–16
   choices for, 4–5
   collaborative approach to, 7
   Desautels on, 2, 5, 6
   description of, xi
   and emotional labeling, 2
   and emotional regulation, 3
   as escape, 2–3
   Greene on, 4, 7
   language for, 2
   mitigating, 6–7
   Perry on, 3
   relationships as prevention of, 7
   structure for, 5
   triggers for, 3
Emotional behavioral disorders (EBDs), 52
Emotional check-ins:

for accountability, 191
for aggression, 145, 146, 151
for anxiety, 22, 111–112, 122, 130
for back talk, 21–23, 29
Brackett on, 111
for bullying, 211, 213, 215–216, 219, 220, 223
Desautels on, 22
for dishonesty, 191–194, 200
for disruptive behavior, 22
for emotional regulation, 79, 151, 152, 155, 211
for helplessness, 71, 72
for inattention, 168, 171, 179
Perry on, 111
personalized, 127, 169
resistance to, 33–34
and restorative practices, 24–25
for school refusal treatment, 41, 50, 56
structured, 32, 35
for triggers, 153
Emotional dysregulation:
and aggression, 135, 155
anxiety as, 105
back talk from, 17
dealing with, 226
disruptive behavior from, 83, 96, 98
Emotional intelligence, x, 3, 184, 205–206, 230
Emotional regulation:
for aggression, 134, 137, 141, 149, 150
for anxiety, 116

of back talk, 25
Brackett on, 162, 230
calm-down strategies for, 10, 32, 93, 103
for dishonesty, 197
for disruptive behavior, 99, 100
and elopement, 3, 4
emotional check-ins for, 79, 151, 152, 155, 211
for helplessness, 59–60, 75
importance of, 142
and mindfulness, 46, 116, 230
monitoring of, 56, 94, 102
separation anxiety as, 98
as shared goal, 145
social emotional learning for, 143
social skills training for, 176, 179
struggles with, 8, 52
student support teams for, 97
support for, 55, 57, 76, 91–93, 101, 155, 202
teaching of, 12, 14, 153–154, 184
for transitions, 57
visual reminders for, 152
Empathy:
for anxiety, 113
and belonging, 24
Brackett on, 18, 205
and bullying, 205–206
in classroom culture, 93, 129
for disruptive behavior, 102
as reactive strategy, 24, 44, 46

Empathy (*continued*)
  as restorative practice, 23–24
  teaching, 50, 120
Empowerment:
  behavior replacement for, 20
  for bullying, 203
  choices for, 138
  coping skills for, 44, 113
  for dishonesty, 199
  and elopement, 5
  for helplessness, 66–67, 74
  restorative practices for, 23, 24
  and self-advocacy, 162
Endorphins, 110–111
Exercise, 110–111. *See also* Movement
Exhaustion, ix, 37, 45, 81, 133, 139, 225–230. *See also* Burnout; Teacher stress
Expectations:
  for anxious students, 112, 128
  for back talk, 26–27
  for calm corners, 11
  and consequences, 206, 220
  consistency of, 84, 87
  for dishonest students, 188, 191–192
  for inattentive students, 161, 167, 172, 175, 176
  modified, 116–117
  of perfection, 119
  and positive reinforcement, 162
  resistance to, 28
  in routines, 137, 164
  setting of, 206
  for teachers, 229
  in teams, 142
Explicit instruction, 62, 72, 166, 179
The Explosive Child (Greene), 4

F

Feedback:
  for aggression, 143
  for anxiety, 126, 128
  for back talk, 25–26, 28, 29
  for bullying, 212
  cues as, 143
  for disruptive behavior, 93, 94, 101, 102
  for helplessness, 62, 78
  for inattention, 160, 162
  parental, 56
  as positive reinforcement, 162
  sentence stems as, 27
Fight, flight, or freeze response, 60, 107, 134
5-4-3-2-1 grounding technique, 117, 118f, 127. *See also* Grounding exercises
Flexibility:
  in accommodations, 111–112
  for anxiety, 113
  in assignments, 116–117
  in attendance, 45, 46
  for disruptive behavior, 86, 96
  for helplessness, 66
  for inattention, 163
  and individualized learning, 44
  in programming, 54

in seating, 86, 96, 161
Fostering Resilient Learners (Souers and Hall), 60, 135
Freeze mode, 60, 114

G
Goodbye rituals, 99–103
Grace, 185, 187
Greene, Ross:
    on aggression, 135, 138
    on anxiety, 112
    on back talk, 18–19, 23
    on dishonesty, 154, 185, 201
    on elopement, 4, 7
Grounding exercises, 55, 126, 128, 137–138, 230. *See also* Breathing exercises; 5-4-3-2-1 grounding technique; Mindfulness
Growth mindset:
    classroom culture of, 67, 70, 73
    development of, 116
    Dweck's work on, 63
    importance of, 77
    lessons for, 119
    parental involvement in, 120, 122
    phrases for, 65
    teaching of, 120
Growth mindset conversation cards, 63*f*

H
Hall, Pete, 60–62, 135, 136, 184, 206, 226, 228
Help card system, 198–200
Helplessness, 59–80
    addressing, 66
    brain training for, 64*f*
    case studies of, 67–80
    causes and triggers of, 60–61
    Desautels on, 60, 62
    emotional regulation for, 59–60
    emotional support for, 64–66
    growth mindset conversation cards for, 63*f*
    multi-step plans for, 61–62
    Perry on, 61, 63
    problem-solving environments for, 61–66
    problem-solving skills for, 62–63
    strategies for, 61–65
    student empowerment for, 66–67
Help-seeking strategies, 198
Honesty, 198–201
Hypervigilance, 149, 158

I
IEPs (Individualized Education Programs), 6–7, 49, 51–54
Impulsive behavior:
    consequences of, 173, 176
    emotional check-ins for, 192, 193
    and executive functioning, 175
    at home, 174, 211
    management of, 18
    neurological causes of, x
    personalized support for, 177
    social skills training for, 176

Impulsive behavior (*continued*)
  stop-and-think strategy for, 175, 176, 178
  in unstructured environments, 173–174, 189, 190
Inattention, 157–179
  as barrier to learning, 157–158
  case studies of, 164–179
  causes of, 158–159
  challenges for, 163
  Desautels on, 158
  functioning skills for, 159–160
  inconsistent progress in, 163
  movement for, 161–162
  peer dynamics in, 163
  positive reinforcement for, 162, 167, 176
  self-advocacy for, 162
  sensory supports for, 160
  strategies for, 159–162
  and time constraints, 163
  visual timers and breaks for, 161
  visually calm environments for, 160–161
Incentives, 46
Individualized Education Programs (IEPs), 6–7, 49, 51–54
Insecurity, 97, 99, 204
Integrity, 198–201

J
Journals, 10, 22, 109, 152

K
Khan Academy, 45

L
Labeling, 2, 10, 33, 184, 185

M
Mentorship, ix, 212, 219, 220
Mindfulness. *See also* Breathing exercises; Grounding exercises
  for aggression, 137, 151
  for anxiety, 109, 113, 116, 119, 129
  for back talk, 22
  and breathing exercises, 42, 117, 127–128, 137, 198, 201
  Desautels on, 42
  for dishonesty, 198–201
  for emotional regulation, 116, 150
  for inattention, 169
  for self-care, 230
Mood meters, 22
Morning buddies, 99
Movement:
  for anxiety, 110–111, 113
  breaks for, 163
  for disruptive behavior, 90–91, 93, 96, 99
  for emotional regulation, 100
  for inattention, 159, 161–162, 174
  sensory supports for, 167
Multi-disciplinary teams, 137, 139
Multi-step plans, 61–62, 67
Multi-Tiered System of Supports (MTSS), 8, 13–14, 16

N

National Bullying Prevention
  Month, 217
Negative thoughts, 42, 109
Neurological differences, 158
Non-verbal cues, 85, 93

O

Open communication, 130, 207,
  208
Outbursts:
  aggressive, 134, 141, 145, 148
  from anxiety, 107
  calm corners for, 146
  description of, xii
  discussions about, 120
  disruptive, 94
  effect on teachers, 226
  intervention for, 153
  from sensory overload, 135
  and trauma, x
  triggers for, 142

P

Paraprofessionals, 50, 54–57, 152
PE, *see* Physical education (PE)
Peer conflicts, 2, 136, 173, 217. *See also*
  Peer pressure; Social dynamics
Peer Influence, 186–187, 212
Peer mediation, 152, 154, 155
Peer pressure, 205. *See also* Peer
  conflicts; Social dynamics
Peer support, 14–15, 86, 220
Perfectionism:
  and anxiety, xii, 105, 106, 114
  Brackett on, 183
  and dishonesty, 183
  and growth mindset, 116
  roots of, 115
  support for, 122
  teaching about, 120
Perry, Bruce:
  on aggression, 134
  on anxiety, 107, 110, 111
  on dishonesty, 182, 185
  on disruptive behavior, 83, 86, 158
  on dysregulated nervous systems, x
  on elopement, 3
  on emotional check-ins, 111
  on helplessness, 61, 63
  on restorative practices, 24
  on self-care, 226
  on trauma, 61
Personalized learning plans, 44
Physical education (PE), 11, 30, 102,
  148–153, 155
Positive reinforcement:
  for accountability, 191–192, 200
  for anxiety, 120
  and attention-seeking, 100
  for back talk, 28
  and bullying, 212, 215–216, 222
  and dishonesty, 186, 192, 194, 200
  for disruptive behavior, 86, 96, 101
  and expectations, 162
  feedback as, 162
  for helplessness, 69, 72–73, 76
  for inattention, 162, 167, 176

Positive reinforcement (*continued*)
  parental, 76
  and responsibility, 176, 191–192
  in routines, 162
Predictability. *See also* Routines; Structured environments
  and aggression, 137, 141
  and anxiety, 108, 127
  Brackett on, 19, 137
  and bullying, 206
  and dishonesty, 183, 184
  and disruptive behavior, 84, 87
  and helplessness, 61, 64–65
  importance of, 5
  and inattention, 175
Proactive strategies. *See also* Reactive strategies
  for aggression, 142, 150, 154
  for anxiety, 107, 113
  for back talk, 20–24
  for behavior replacement, 4, 20–21
  for breathing, 109, 137
  for bullying, 209
  and choices, 4–5
  for disruptive behavior, 84
  for elopement, 4–5, 7, 9, 12, 15
  and emotional check-ins, 21–23
  for helplessness, 61
  in high-risk situations, 151
  for inattention, 166
  MTSS framework as, 8
  power of, 46
  reactive strategies vs., 44–46
  restorative practices as, 23–24

  in structured environments, 5
  for unmet needs, 135
Problem-solvers walls, 70
Proximity, 85
Pushout (Couvson), 135

Q
Quality Over Speed concept, 26, 28

R
Reactive strategies, 23, 44–46, 142. *See also* Proactive strategies
Redirection, xii, 85, 97, 117, 207
Reentry plans, 53–56
Reintegration, 44–46
Relaxation spaces, 126, 127. *See also* Calm down corners; Safe zones
Respectful communication, 27, 28, 32, 34, 84, 221. *See also* Active listening
Responsibility. *See also* Accountability
  avoidance of, 183
  and dishonesty, 196, 197
  importance of, 193
  monitoring of, 200
  positive reinforcement for, 176, 191–192
  restorative practices for, 23
  safe spaces for, 190
  SEL lessons for, 188
  social stories for, 190
Restorative circles, 19, 154
Restorative conversations, 19, 23, 193, 198–201

Restorative practices, 19, 23–25, 140, 154, 191, 194, 196

Role-playing:
- for anxiety, 127
- for back talk, 22, 33
- for bullying, 206, 211, 213, 221
- for dishonesty, 194, 198, 199
- for helplessness, 70

Routines. *See also* Predictability; Structured environments
- for aggression, 137
- for anxiety, 108
- for back talk, 34
- of breathing exercises, 109
- changes in, 31, 135
- for dishonesty, 187, 195
- for disruptive behavior, 84, 99
- for emotional check-ins, 32, 111
- of goodbye rituals, 99–103
- for helplessness, 65
- for inattention, 163, 165, 172
- and positive reinforcement, 162
- SEL lessons as, 145, 188, 214
- for self-care, 230

RULER framework, 84, 184–185

Runners, 1, 2

S

Safe zones, 151. *See also* Calm down corners; Relaxation spaces

School refusal, 37–58
- Brackett on, 37–38
- and bullying, 37
- case studies of, 46–58
- Desautels on, 38, 40
- description of, xi–xii
- emotional regulation in, 38
- mindfulness in, 42–44
- reactive strategies for, 44–46
- stakeholders' role in, 40–42
- supportive relationships for, 38
- triggers of, 55
- 2x10 strategy for, 39–40
- understanding, 37–38
- warning signs of, 39–44

School refusal treatment:
- accommodations for, 42
- coping skills for, 44
- emotional check-ins for, 41, 50, 56
- empathy in, 38
- feedback in, 56
- flexibility in, 44
- mindfulness in, 42–44, 46
- positive reinforcement in, 54
- proactive strategies for, 37–39
- in structured environments, 46

School-based therapy, 55

SEL, *see* Social Emotional Learning (SEL)

Self-advocacy, 162, 168, 169, 171

Self-care, 87, 139, 227–230
- Desautels on, 87
- Perry on, 226

Self-esteem, 75, 99, 100, 103, 183, 204

Self-regulation charts, 168–171

Self-regulation skills:
  for anxiety, 128
  for dishonesty, 189, 192, 195
  for disruptive behavior, 103
  5-4-3-2-1 grounding technique in, 103
  for inattention, xiii, 165, 166
  for teachers, 87
Sensory breaks, 86, 90–95, 167, 171
Sensory overload, 2, 3, 83, 135
Sensory processing difficulties, 157, 159, 164, 166
Sensory supports, 159, 160, 166–168, 175, 177
Sentence stems, 20, 21f, 27–30, 32–34
Separation anxiety, 39, 98–99
Siegel, Dan, 107, 145
Sleep deprivation, 159
Social dynamics, 3, 136. *See also* Peer conflicts; Peer pressure
Social Emotional Learning (SEL):
  for accountability, 195–197
  for aggression, 138–139, 143, 145, 146
  for bullying, 206, 214
  definition of, 138–139
  for dishonesty, 193, 198–200
  for inattention, 163
  for responsibility, 188
  as routine, 145, 188, 214
Social Isolation, 37, 111, 112, 122, 140, 148, 163, 210
Social media, 216, 219, 222
Social skills:
  development of, 49, 52
  support for, 126
  training for, 176, 177, 179
Social skills groups, 127, 129–130, 212, 215–216, 222
Social work sessions, 55
Souers, Kristin, xiii
Square breathing, 201. *See also* Breathing exercises
SSTs, *see* Student support teams (SSTs)
Stakeholders, 40–42, 46, 138, 173
Stigma, 10, 15, 33, 120, 140, 143, 163
Stop and think strategy, 175–178
Stop sign cards, 152, 153
Structured environments. *See also* Predictability; Routines; Unstructured environments
  affirmations in, 109
  for aggression, 146
  for anxiety, 108, 130
  for back talk, 25, 32, 33
  breaks as, 161
  breathing mats as, 110f
  for bullying, 209, 211
  for dishonesty, 191, 195, 199
  for disruptive behavior, 88, 90, 96, 101
  for elopement, 4
  of emotional check-ins, 32, 35
  expectations in, 162
  for gradual integration, 45–46
  for helplessness, 65, 75
  importance of, 108

for inattention, 169, 172–173
MTSS framework as, 8
physical education as, 151, 153
restorative circles as, 19
school refusal treatment in, 46
for sensory breaks, 92
social skills groups in, 212
student input in, 5
think-alouds as, 62
for transitions, 99
for triggers, 127
Structured recess activities, 152, 175–177, 179, 188
Student engagement, 85–86
Student support teams (SSTs), 68, 74, 89, 94, 97–99, 102, 103
Supervision, 6, 99, 152, 153, 189, 211, 219–220
Support networks, xiv, 230

T
Tapping out, 227–228
Tapping-out strategy, 227–228
Teacher stress, 83, 87. *See also* Burnout; Exhaustion
Think-alouds, 62
Tier 1 approach, 8, 12, 42, 107
Traffic light system, 143
Trauma:
  and aggression, 150
  assessment of, 40
  and bullying, 204–205
  and dishonesty, 182, 183
  and disruptive behavior, 83, 86
  and dysregulated nervous systems, x
  and emotional dysregulation, 135
  and emotional regulation, 3
  and helplessness, 60–61
  and inattention, 157–158
  -informed teaching, 83
  Perry on, 61
  and stress, 158–159
  support for, 139
  vicarious, xiv, 225–226
Triggers:
  accommodations for, 112
  of aggression, 133–136, 141, 142
  of anxiety, 115, 120
  and avoidance behavior, 107
  of back talk, 20, 31
  as behavioral causes, 2
  of bullying, 204–205, 220, 221
  from competition, 152, 153
  of dishonesty, 182–183
  documenting, 125
  of elopement, 3, 20
  emotional regulation for, 137
  of helplessness, 60–61, 67
  from hypervigilance, 149
  identifying, 144–146, 174
  of inattention, 158–159
  management of, 126, 127
  parental insights into, 53
  from separation anxiety, 98
  from trauma, 123
  in unstructured time, 211
2x10 strategy, 39–40, 41*f*, 46, 48, 52, 55–56, 136

U

University of Florida Literacy Institute, 45
Unmet needs, 2, 4, 17, 20, 81, 90, 135, 204
Unstructured environments. *See also* Structured environments
  aggression in, 148, 150
  art classes as, 117
  behavior contracts for, 219, 220, 223
  bullying in, 209, 211, 215, 217
  dishonesty in, 188, 189, 193, 195
  elopement in, 13
  impulsive behavior in, 190
  inattention in, 174–175, 182–173
  supervision during, 219
  support during, 212
Upstairs brain, 145

V

Venet, Alex Shevrin, 19
Verbal cues, 143–144
Vicarious trauma, xiv, 225–226
Visual cues, 143–144, 152, 153, 167, 168, 192
Visual timers, 10, 127, 161, 163, 167
Vulnerability, 136, 182, 185–186, 218, 226

W

Withdrawn behavior, 107
Wlodkowski, Raymond, 39, 48

Y

Yale Center for Emotional Intelligence, x, 2, 18, 37, 84, 184